TAKING DRUGS SERIOUSLY

James Kay and Julian Cohen are nationally known figures in drug education. They are health education specialists with a wide knowledge of health issues and extensive experience of working with young people and parents. James Kay currently manages Healthwise, a health information service in Liverpool, and sits on government advisory bodies on drug abuse; Julian Cohen used to co-ordinate a drugs education project in Greater Manchester and now works as a freelance trainer and writer. He is the author of a number of drugs education packs for young people.

Taking Drugs Seriously

*A Parent's Guide to
Young People's Drug Use*

Julian Cohen and James Kay

Thorsons
An Imprint of HarperCollins*Publishers*

Thorsons
An Imprint of HarperCollins*Publishers*
77–85 Fulham Palace Road
Hammersmith, London W6 8JB
1160 Battery Street
San Francisco, California 94111–1213
Published by Thorsons 1994

10 9 8 7 6 5 4 3 2

A catalogue record for this book
is available from the British Library

ISBN 0 7225 2858 2

Printed in Great Britain by
HarperCollins Manufacturing Glasgow

We would like to dedicate this book to our children
Beth, Michelle, Robert and Stuart.

CONTENTS

Part III: Coping in a crisis

Part IV: Conclusion

Appendix I: Facts about drugs

Appendix II: Where to find out more

ACKNOWLEDGEMENTS

We would like to thank the following people who have helped us with the book:

Helen Galley for her tireless work on the manuscript.

The staff and volunteers at Healthwise for their support in all our work with parents and young people.

The staff from the Mersey Drug Training and Information Unit for their helpful comments on a draft of the book.

The parents we have worked with over the years and, more recently, those who looked at earlier drafts of the book.

Any errors are of course the sole responsibility of the authors.

INTRODUCTION

• *'Drug cocktail kills teenager'* • *'11 year old junkies'* •
'Drugs in city centre club' • *'Sharp rise in drug seizures'*
• *'New drug danger warning'* •

The media headlines about young people's drug use are endless. It can all seem very scary for parents. To make matters worse, a lot of youngsters are very casual about it all and just don't understand why their parents get so worried.

This book aims to help you understand young people's drug use. It is based on the latest information about drugs and the latest research into drug use in the UK. It contains lots of practical advice about what you can actually do as a parent, whether your youngster is using drugs or not.

We want to emphasize right at the beginning that there is no need to become over-alarmed about young people's drug use. When you sift the myths from the facts and take a calm look at what young people are up to, it is not all doom and gloom.

Of course there are real dangers from drug use, but it is important to keep them in perspective. We ourselves try to take a calm, balanced and practical approach to the subject. We have both worked with parents and youngsters about drug use and are both parents. We share the concerns of parents for their youngsters and we hope that this book reflects the reality of what being a parent is like today.

The book is divided into six main sections:

Part I: This gives information about some of the main questions parents ask about young people's drug use. We have tried to answer questions honestly and in a practical way.

Part II: This focuses on what every parent can do, whether their youngster uses drugs or not. It includes activities for both parents and youngsters to work through, as well as information.

Part III: This gives advice on coping in a crisis – when you suspect or know your youngster is actually using drugs or has been arrested, suspended from school, etc.

Part IV: A short conclusion summarizing some of the main points in the book.

Appendix I: This is a reference section which gives detailed information about drugs themselves. It includes information on the effects and risks of using different drugs.

Appendix II: This contains information on helping organizations, books, pamphlets, computer programs and other drug education resources to use at home and/or with education groups.

How to use this book

This book can be used in several ways. You can read it through from cover to cover or just dip into it, picking out the bits you are most interested in. It can be used as a reference book to check out particular pieces of information. You can also turn to it for advice in a crisis.

You can read through the book by yourself but you can also go through all, or some of it, with your partner, a friend or your youngster(s). It contains activities which are designed to be used by you and your youngster working together. We want to encourage you to do this if you can. The book is based on the PACT principle – Parents And Children Talking. We believe that there is a need for much

more talking and listening between parents and their
youngsters on the drugs issue.

We hope you find it useful.

Last, but not least, we value your views about this book,
ways it could be improved and any other ideas you have
about educating parents about drugs. If you wish to contact us, write to:

Parents Drugs Education
c/o Healthwise, 9 Slater Street , Liverpool L1 4BW, UK

Part I

● ●

Questions parents ask
about young people's
drug use

● ●

1: HOW BIG A PROBLEM IS IT?

It can be very difficult to know how seriously to take the problem of drug use. Stories in the media seem to suggest a tidal wave of drug use sweeping over the country. Everybody seems to be at it. Then it all goes quiet for a while before once again the media are full of it.

How likely is it that your youngster will come across drug use at their school or down your street? What are the chances that they will actually use drugs? If they do use drugs, which drugs are they likely to be? Above all, how dangerous is it really?

There are no quick answers to these questions but recent surveys and research into patterns of drug use amongst young people provide a useful starting-point. Much of the survey information cited below is reported in *Drug Misuse in Britain 1992* published by The Institute for the Study of Drug Dependence. We also report on research conducted in Liverpool and the Wirral in 1992.

How many are using what?

The drug most commonly used by young people is *caffeine*, which is in tea, coffee, many soft drinks and some chocolates. The second most commonly used drug is *alcohol*. Surveys show that by the age of 16 well over 95 per cent of youngsters have had an alcoholic drink and that over a third are regular weekly drinkers. Young males are more likely to drink alcohol than females and more likely to drink larger quantities. Recent reports, however, suggest that girls may be catching up as time goes on.

Much under-age drinking takes place in pubs and as many as two thirds of 16 to 17 year olds will have illegally purchased alcohol. It is often easier for young girls, rather than boys, to drink in pubs and clubs, because they tend to look older.

The third most popular drug of choice amongst young people is *tobacco*. Just under a third of 16 year olds smoke on a daily basis. A slightly higher proportion of young females smoke than young males. Smoking is also class related. Smoking rates amongst middle-class people are lower than amongst their working-class counterparts. The growth market for the cigarette manufacturers seems to be working-class young women.

The extent of the use of illegal drugs and solvents is more difficult to establish. This is because young people are often careful to conceal their use of illicit drugs. Also, patterns of illegal drug use amongst young people vary between different places and over time, while levels of alcohol and cigarette use tend to be similar in different areas. But by putting together surveys and research projects that were carried out in different parts of the UK in the late 1980s and early 1990s, we can develop a general picture:

1. More young people are coming into contact with illegal drugs. A recent study of 14 to 15 year olds in Manchester and Liverpool found 59 per cent claiming they had been offered an illegal drug, solvents or poppers (liquid gold or nitrites).

2. The age of first use and first contact with illegal drugs seems to be going down.

3. More young people are actually using illegal drugs. In some areas a majority of 16 year olds may have tried an illegal drug or solvents at least once.

4. Whilst the extent of use varies from area to area, what is striking is how widespread the use of some drugs is. Drugs are not only available in inner city

areas. Young people and drugs both travel easily. The leafy suburbs and rural areas also have their fill of young people using drugs.

5. In the past there have been higher rates of illegal drug use amongst males than females. However, some recent surveys have suggested that, at the same age, more young females than males may be experimenting with illegal drugs. This may be because girls 'mature' earlier, mix with boys who are older and so come into contact with drugs at an earlier age than boys. They also are more likely to get into pubs and clubs at a younger age.

6. The most commonly used illegal drug is *cannabis*. Survey suggest that there are over a million regular users in the UK and that as many as 2–3 million people have used it. (Many of these people are now themselves parents.) The Manchester and Liverpool survey of 14 to 15 year olds found just under a third claiming to have used cannabis. Other studies have also given figures of over 25 per cent.

   Most studies show that experimenting with illegal drugs increases in the later teen years. In some communities use of cannabis is seen as normal and will include use by parents as well as teenagers.

7. The most recent increases in drug use amongst young people have been linked to the popularity of the dance club and rave scene. This has combined particular types of music, dancing and fashion with the use of drugs like ecstasy, amphetamine, LSD and cannabis.

Looking at the individual drugs, there are some more points that we can make:

Amphetamine – This drug has a long history of use in the UK. There has been a recent revival of interest in its use alongside the ecstasy scene. Local surveys show 5 to 10 per cent of 15 to 16 year olds claim to have used it at least once.

Cocaine (and crack, a form of cocaine) – The use and availability of this drug is not nearly as common as the media would have us believe. The predicted American-style crack cocaine epidemic has not happened in the UK. Cocaine and crack are available in some areas but are very expensive and thus outside the experience of most younger people. Local surveys of 14 to 16 year olds show that less than 1 per cent have used. Figures may be slightly higher for older teenagers in some areas.

Ecstasy – This has become the most popular drug on the dance club and rave scene. It has been estimated that there are tens of thousands of young people using ecstasy and similar drugs, mainly at weekends. In the Manchester/Liverpool survey of 14 to 15 year olds, 6 per cent claimed they had used ecstasy at least once. A 1992 national survey of 15 to 24 year olds found 7 per cent claiming they had used it. The most recent 1992 survey in Liverpool and the Wirral showed 12 per cent of 15 to 20 year olds claiming to have used it at least once.

Heroin (and other opiate drugs) – Again, despite all the media hype, use of heroin by young people is relatively rare. In local surveys of 14 to 16 year olds usually less than 1 per cent claim to have ever used heroin. The figures may be slightly higher for older teenagers in some inner city areas.

LSD – This was a popular 'hippy' drug in the 1960s. It

went out of fashion, but from the late 1980s onwards has again become popular. In surveys, 5 to 13 per cent of 14 to 16 year olds claim to have used it at least once.

Magic mushrooms – These are particularly popular in late summer and early autumn when they grow wild in many areas. Surveys have found that 5 to 15 per cent of 15 to 16 year olds claim to have used them at least once.

Poppers (nitrites, liquid gold) – These are available from sex and joke shops and clubs. They are not illegal to use or to sell. They were used mainly by gay men but now their use by young people in general is more common. One survey put the number of 14 to 15 year olds claiming to have used at least once at 14 per cent. Few studies have asked youngsters about their use of this drug.

Solvents – This is the inhaling or sniffing of glues, butane gas, aerosols, etc. Use tends to vary greatly from area to area and from time to time. Recently there has been a switch away from the use of glue to the more dangerous use of gas and aerosols. Local surveys show up to 20 per cent of 15 to 16 year olds using solvents at least once.

Steroids – Used medically for a number of complaints; there has now been an increase in their non-medical use. They are used by sports people and body-builders and increasingly by young people who want a 'beautiful body'. This may include the 'health and fitness' types of youngsters who are not normally associated with drug use. How widespread use of steroids is is not known for sure, but it is definitely on the increase.

Tranquillizers – About 14 per cent of British adults
take these drugs on prescription at some time in
each year. Young people, especially girls, are
prescribed them for anxiety. There is also a street
trade in tranquillizers. Some youngsters use the
tablets, often combined with alcohol, to get a buzz.
We do not know how widespread this is. Also some
injectors of opiate-type drugs such as heroin use
tranquillizers (especially temazepam) if they cannot
get heroin. This is very rare amongst the younger
age groups.

Finding out more about drug use in your area

So far we have described the general picture. It will vary
from area to area. If you want more information about
drug use in your locality there are a few places you can go
to get the information.

A good place to start is your local library. The larger central libraries will have the most information, but even
branch libraries should have some leaflets and contact
information. They may be able to tell you about local drug
agencies and projects and may have copies of any local surveys into drug use which have been published. They might
also have a press cuttings file on drug use.

Most specialist drug agencies are happy to talk to the
'worried well' and will have a pretty clear idea about what
proportions of local youth are using which drugs. However,
it is worth remembering that many specialist agencies deal
with very heavy users of drugs like heroin. They may not
be as knowledgeable about younger users of drugs like
ecstasy, cannabis, etc.

Your Local Education Authority may have specialist

health education advisers and youth workers who have done a lot of work on drug issues. You should be able to contact them through the education department and they may be able to tell you more.

Also there is a national network of new Regional Health Information Services, which were set up under the Patients Charter system. They are available on a free phone number: 0800 66 55 44. When you ring this number you are automatically switched through to your local service. Some are open for longer hours than others, but all should be open from 9.00 to 5.00 Monday to Friday. They should be able to help you in your quest for further local information about drug use.

Two final suggestions: ask other local parents and young people (and most of all your own youngster) about what they think goes on locally; also look at page 96, 'Know where and how to get help in your area' and Appendix II, 'Where to find out more', page 165.

But is it a problem?

Drug use is now widespread among young people. There are large minorities of teenagers and young adults using a wide range of drugs. There are very few teenagers in Britain today who do not at least know a friend or schoolmate who has used illegal drugs. Even those who choose not to use illegal drugs themselves will probably come across them at some time.

How worried should we be about this situation? How dangerous is it really? We need to emphasize that in the vast majority of cases, use of drugs by young people does not lead to serious problems. To get matters in perspective, it helps to understand that many young people will only use occasionally, or for a short period, and then decide to stop. Others will use more regularly and take care about what they do, much as many responsible adults use alcohol. There *are* young people who get into health, social, financial or legal problems with drug use, but these are a small minority.

For more information about the different ways young people use drugs, see 'Why do young people use drugs?', page 10. 'What effects do drugs have and what are the real dangers?', page 26, describes some of the general risks of drug use, and Appendix I, 'Facts about drugs', page 127, outlines some of the specific risks associated with use of individual drugs.

Drug use is certainly risky – and certain drugs and ways of taking them are more risky than others. About 300 mainly young people die as a result of using illegal drugs each year. About another 150 die as a result of solvent use. Every one of these deaths is a tragedy, but they need to be set alongside the 300 people a *day* who die in the UK from the effects of smoking cigarettes. That is about 100,000 a year. Some health experts have estimated that more people die each year from the effects of passive tobacco smoking than from heroin use. There are also another 20,000 to 30,000 a year whose deaths are associated with alcohol use. Whilst few of the tobacco-related deaths directly involve young people, a significant number of alcohol-related deaths do.

Of course, very few parents are happy to see their son or daughter taking illegal drugs and there has rightly been much concern about recent increases in drug use by young people. The good news for us, as parents, is that only in a small minority of cases does it lead to serious harm. One task we set ourselves in this book is to help you to reduce this number further.

2: WHY DO YOUNG PEOPLE USE DRUGS?

Young people use drugs in different ways. Some use drugs only for a short time, possibly only once or twice. These are the *experimenters*. Some go on from experimenting to use the drug in a regular but fairly controlled way, taking care what they use, how much and how often. These are the *recreational* users. A small group of youngsters will come to rely on the feelings that their drug use gives them to help them through their day. They will not be able to do without their drugs for long. These we call *dependent* drug users.

These are important distinctions to make. Why a youngster experiments with drugs will be very different from why they use in a recreational or dependent way.

Experimentation

Think about the reasons why young people might experiment with drugs.

- ~ *Drugs are available.* They are there to use – why not have a go?

- ~ *Out of boredom.* Nothing better to do – why not have a go, when it might be fun?

- ~ *Out of curiosity.* It sounds interesting – why not see what it makes you feel like?

- ~ *Pressure from other people.* Everybody else is doing it and you don't want to be the odd one out – it's good to be 'one of the crowd' or part of the 'in set'.

- ~ *As a protest.* You know you shouldn't, but it's fun to rebel sometimes, especially doing things your parents would not approve of – naughty but nice.

None of these reasons reveal any great social or psychological problem in the young drug experimenter. They are all the sort of everyday reasons why young people take risks with other things they shouldn't do or which put them in danger – things like stealing from shops, riding motorbikes, using skateboards, joining gangs and playing chicken with traffic. Some of these things are dangerous, illegal and/or downright stupid. But other risky activities are encouraged by most adults as healthy sport. Young people die each year and thousands are injured in sports like football, rugby, climbing, swimming, cycling, canoeing, abseiling, etc.

Taking risks, experimenting with new situations and changing the way you feel are normal parts of growing up. Most of the time young people get away with it.

Recreation

Those who go on to use recreationally are getting something else out of their drug use. The reasons why they started using are listed above. They carry on using because they get something they particularly value out of the drug use.

We are so used to talking about the problems of drugs that it can seem strange to talk about the pleasures or benefits. Yet this is what we have to do, if we want to understand why young people use drugs regularly in a recreational way.

~ It's fun. Using drugs can make you feel happy,
   relaxed, sexy and sometimes full of energy.

~ Some drug use fits in well with other social activities
   and fashions that young people like, such as dancing
   or listening to music. The drug effect can enhance
   the pleasure.

~ Drugs like ecstasy, LSD and cannabis don't have the
nasty hangover effects you get from similar
amounts of alcohol. They are a much nicer 'buzz',
according to many young people.

~ These days many drugs are cheaper – or at least as
cheap – as alcohol.

This begins to sound like an advert for drugs. If it's that
good, shouldn't we keep quiet about it or we'll have even
more youngsters using?

This is a key problem for parents to understand. The
uncomfortable truth is that in moderation and for most
young people, drug use is fun and pleasurable and does not
lead to many problems. That is why we have tens of thousands using ecstasy every weekend and maybe a million or
more smoking cannabis each year. We do no one any
favours by avoiding the truth or doctoring it in some way
to make it seem worse. We have a big gap in understanding
between adults and young people on drugs. Most of that
gap is caused by our reluctance to recognize that from the
young person's point of view, these can be very attractive
substances, whether we like it or not.

Dependency

A small minority of those who use drugs will become
dependent on the drug experience as a way of getting
through life. These are the ones who are often called
'addicts'. They tend to be dependent on the heavy sedative
drugs like alcohol, heroin and barbiturates, although
dependency on other drug types is possible. The reasons
why some people become dependent on drugs are very different from the reasons for experimentation or recreational use.

The reasons for dependency can include:

~ The drug use blocks out physical pain. Some dependent users started using in hospital, after operations, but this is rare among younger people.

~ The drug use can block out psychological pain. Many people have become dependent on tranquillizers after being prescribed them to cope with the death of a loved one. Others may use alcohol or heroin to block out negative emotions and feelings about themselves, their situation or past experiences. Drug use may 'cocoon' them from what they experience as a very unpleasant world.

~ Life can seem dull and empty – particularly if you are poor, unemployed and maybe living in bad housing. What is the point of it? Drug use can float you away, make you forget your day-to-day worries.

~ The daily hustle to make money, score drugs, avoid the police and be part of a drug scene with other people can provide some structure and apparent meaning to an otherwise empty life.

As you can see, these reasons are all much more to do with the physical, social and emotional needs of young people. This sort of drug use is a retreat into the safety and predictability of the drug use experience. This is quite unlike the reaching out into a new and exciting lifestyle that experimenters or recreational users are looking for.

In summary

What can we make of all of this? An early step, when you are looking at what might be drug use in a young person, is

to try and work out what is going on for them. What sort of
drug use is it? Remember that drug use is a very individual
thing and varies depending on the person and their situation. Take care not to jump to conclusions or make assump-
tions about young people in general and your youngsters in
particular. Talk to them, listen to them and get to understand their concerns (you'll find ideas on how to do this in
Part II).

Many parents blame themselves or other people if their
youngsters use drugs. Remember that drug use is very
common amongst young people and can seem a 'normal
thing' from their point of view. In many areas there are
large minorities of young people who have experimented
with illegal drugs. Most young people use drugs because
they want to and out of their own choice, without being
forced to do so.

● ●
3: WHERE DO YOUNG PEOPLE GET
   DRUGS FROM?

The drug pusher myth

There is a popular image of the evil drug dealer plying
unsuspecting and innocent young people with dangerous
drugs. In its most scary form this image has the drug
dealer in an ice-cream van outside the school gates dispens-
ing heroin over the counter.

Thankfully this almost never happens. Offering drugs to
new 'customers' is a risky business. They might tell someone and the maximum sentence for supplying illegal drugs
is life imprisonment. Imagine the treatment a drug dealer
would receive from the judge if the offence involved selling
direct to youngsters in such a way. Worse still for them,

imagine if local parents got hold of them! Even drug dealers have more sense than to run such risks for the chance of making a small amount of new business.

Another myth about the supply of drugs is that dealers will somehow spike the drinks, ice-creams or sweets of young people in order to get them hooked on the drugs. The idea is that they will then go on to charge higher prices to make up for the earlier losses. Again this is very unlikely once you think about how this actually might take place. It assumes:

... that dealers have spare supplies for such speculations.
... that the spiked young people would know what was
    making them feel strange.
... that they wouldn't tell anyone else about how they
    were feeling.
... that they would come back to the dealer, money in
    hand and anxious to repeat the experience.

Young people, however, do sometimes spike each others' drinks and/or drugs. It is a stupid and dangerous thing to do but they do it 'for a laugh', not to get a novice 'hooked' on the experience.

Your mate – the dealer

The truth is that young people usually get drugs in small quantities from friends, older brothers and sisters, other relations or acquaintances. This was confirmed in recent research in Liverpool where we found that over 50 per cent of young people questioned told us that they got illegal drugs 'from a mate'. Less than 10 per cent used a dealer.

This is because in most cases drugs are not *pushed* at all but *pulled*. One person gets hold of some drugs and other young people scrounge some off them, ask them for them or are thankful to be offered some. Somebody in almost every school, youth club or group of young people will know someone who knows someone who can get drugs in this way. Another way it happens is for a group of young people to pool their money and one of them, who knows someone who has some drugs, buys for the group.

Of course there are larger scale drug dealers, but they tend to avoid younger people. Youngsters tend to be poor customers with their limited incomes and tendency to tell tales. If young people do come into direct contact with 'dealers' these are likely to be small scale local dealers who are probably users themselves.

There used to be a clear distinction between suppliers of drugs like cannabis and LSD and those who sold heroin. With the increase in the variety of drugs these days it is not clear whether that distinction still always holds good. Some people argue that cannabis should be legally supplied so that young people could get hold of it easily without having to make contact with people who might supply them with more dangerous drugs like heroin. Whatever the merits of this case, it seems unlikely to happen in the foreseeable future.

How much does it cost?

The answer is: not nearly as much as many parents think. If young people are looking for a good night out with their mates they can get it as cheap, or cheaper, using illegal drugs than they can with alcohol. In 1993 in Liverpool and Manchester £10 spent on cannabis could buy enough to make three or four joints (cannabis cigarettes). This is enough for a small group of people to get a good high. The same amount will buy half a tablet of ecstasy, a 'bag' of amphetamine or heroin. At £2.50–£4 a tablet, LSD is very cheap. One tablet can give up to 10–12 hours 'tripping'. Illegal drugs have become cheaper compared to the cost of alcohol. Given these prices, it is not too surprising that more and more young people are using illegal drugs.

●●●●●●●●●●●●●●●●●●●●●●●●●●●●●●●●●●●●●●●

4: WHAT DOES ALL THIS DRUG LANGUAGE MEAN?

The language of drugs can seem strange and difficult to understand for many parents. On the one hand there is the obscure technical jargon of the medical profession and others who work helping drug users; on the other, the strange street jargon of the drug 'scene' that so many young people use.

Medical/drug professionals' terms

We have given below a short glossary of terms that doctors and drug specialists might use and terms that are in wide popular use.

You might want to start by thinking about what you understand by the following terms:

addiction	overdose
dependency	problem drug taker
depressant	psychoactive
drug	psychotropic
drug abuse	sedative
drug misuse	soft drugs
hallucinogenic	stimulant
hard drugs	tolerance
hypnotic	withdrawal symptoms
narcotic	

We define these terms as follows:

addiction This term is usually applied to drugs but can be used with lots of activities that can become compulsive habits – like gambling or playing arcade games. With drugs it means someone who uses on an everyday basis and finds it difficult to stop using. The term 'workaholic' has been used to describe people addicted to work. The term 'addiction' is not used so often now by professionals because it has come to mean so many things to different people. It can also conjure up misleading stereotypes of drug users. Many prefer the more precise term *dependency* (see below).

dependency Drug dependency is usually divided into *physical* and *psychological*.

Physical dependency is when someone has taken drugs in quantity for a time and comes to rely on the use of a drug in order to feel well and for their body to function 'normally'. It is often found when the body has built up a *tolerance* (see page 21) to the drug and in its absence physical *withdrawal symptoms* (see page 21) appear. It can only happen with certain drugs, especially *depressant* drugs like alcohol, barbiturates, heroin or tranquillizers.

Psychological dependency is when the user experiences an overwhelming desire to continue with the drug experience. This can be because of the pleasurable effects, but is more likely to represent some sort of psychological crutch. The drug experience has become a way of blocking out reality, of making life bearable, of facing the world. Without the crutch life seems worthless. This can happen with any drug.

depressant This describes a drug which depresses or

slows down the operation of the central nervous system. Alcohol, heroin and tranquillizers are depressants.

drug There are many different definitions of drug, here we use the term for any substance which, when taken into the body, changes the way you think or feel.

drug abuse Drug abuse is a term very widely used but rarely defined. It seems to be used most often to describe drug use that is not liked by society or by individuals. The problem is that societies and individuals change their minds from time to time about what sorts of drug use is OK. We try to avoid using this term because one person's use seems to be another person's abuse.

drug misuse This term is very much like *drug abuse* above and with all its shortcomings. It is sometimes used to mean the illegal use of drugs.

hallucinogenic This describes a drug which alters perception: the way you see, hear, feel, smell or touch the world. This can mean that these senses can get all mixed up or changed. You may see colours much more brightly perhaps or hear sounds differently. LSD and so-called magic mushrooms are hallucinogenic drugs; the term is also sometimes used to describe ecstasy.

hard drugs This term has been used to describe what are believed to be the most dangerous drugs such as heroin and cocaine. It is not a term most drug specialists would use because it is too vague. For example is amphetamine a hard drug or not? Some would say yes, others no, still others would say it depends on how it is taken, how much is taken, etc.

hypnotic This term is used to describe drugs which help you to sleep – sometimes whether you want to or not! Examples are barbiturates and tranquillizers, although other depressant drugs like alcohol and heroin can also have this effect.

narcotic This comes from a Greek word meaning 'to numb'. It is a bit of an old-fashioned word now but has been used in two ways: firstly to describe drugs that have an hypnotic effect – i.e. those that make you sleepy – secondly in a more general way to describe so-called *hard drugs* like heroin and cocaine.

overdose This means, as it sounds, taking more of the drug than is necessary to get an effect. It is an over dose. In some cases it can be harmful or even fatal, particularly with *sedative* drugs like barbiturates, heroin or alcohol.

problem drug taker This term is used by drug specialists to describe anyone who has a problem with their use of drugs. The problems could be legal, physical, psychological or social.

psychoactive This refers to drugs which are active in the psyche or mind – in other words, the type of drugs we discuss in this book.

psychotropic This means virtually the same as *psychoactive*. It is a good example of medical jargon – two obscure words for the same thing.

sedative This is similar to *depressant*. It refers to drugs which sedate or depress the central nervous system. They slow things down. Heroin, alcohol, tranquillizers – these are all sedative drugs.

soft drugs A term sometimes used to describe drugs like cannabis which cannot result in physical *dependency*. It is contrasted with *hard drugs*, which are generally believed to be much more dangerous. Like the term 'hard drugs', it is a bit vague because people can still have problems using so-called 'soft drugs'. Many drug specialists will not use the term for that reason.

stimulant This describes drugs which tend to stimulate or speed up the action of the central nervous system. They are almost the opposite of *sedative* or *depressant* drugs. Amphetamine (sometimes called speed or whizz), cocaine, caffeine and ecstasy are all stimulant drugs.

tolerance This is the process by which the body can adapt to the presence of a drug such that you need to take more to get the same effect. The body learns to tolerate the drug in the system. Alcohol, barbiturates, heroin and amphetamine are all drugs to which the body can build up tolerance.

withdrawal symptoms These are usually described as a series of symptoms (a syndrome) which can be caused by stopping the use of a drug to which the body has become *tolerant*. As the body learns to adapt to the drug, it becomes reliant on the drug just to feel normal. Take the drug away and you feel terrible – until the body readjusts back to its normal drug-free functioning. Withdrawal symptoms usually take the form of shivering, shaking, aching joints, running nose and similar 'flu-like symptoms.

What about the street language?

Like many other social activities, drug use has its own jargon. Special words have been developed by drug users to describe the drugs, methods of use and other activities involving drug use. This street slang can be fairly obscure as in 'dropping love doves' (taking ecstasy tablets) or 'cranking smack' (injecting heroin). We have included some of the slang words for different drugs in Appendix I, 'Facts about drugs', page 127, to help you understand what is being talked about. But there are some pitfalls to avoid.

Street slang changes – sometimes rapidly. This is partly because it changes when the terms become more widely known. Just when parents and teachers think they have learnt the latest terms they find they are out-of-date. After all, the purpose of street language is to communicate without people like parents and teachers knowing what is going on. Although some terms live for decades, there are others which survive for only a few weeks.

Also, some slang terms mean different things in different places. 'Dope', for example, can mean cannabis or sometimes heroin. In some places it means all illegal drugs and in others underground intelligence about what drugs are available on the street. 'Give me the dope' could therefore have at least four potential meanings.

Young drug users themselves are sometimes confused about slang and make mistakes. This is because they want to be seen by their friends as being 'in the know'. We recently came across a young person using the term 'trips' to mean either LSD, ecstasy or amphetamine. By the way they used the term it was apparent that they did not know they were describing three different drugs or that 'trip' is most often used to describe the experience of taking LSD. We have also found young people using 'draw' without realizing that they were using cannabis or that it was an offence to be in possession of it.

We suggest that you take care using street language. Nothing can be worse than using last year's slang in the mistaken belief that it makes you sound 'hip'. Here are a few guidelines:

~ Wherever possible, use the proper name for the drug rather than the slang word – i.e. heroin not smack – unless you are very comfortable with the slang.

~ If a young person uses a slang term, check out that you have understood it properly: 'Do you mean amphetamine?' 'Do you mean injecting?' and so on. Most young people will be more than happy to explain it to you. They can be like most hobbyists explaining their interest to someone new.

~ As always,.the key is *communication*. Listen to your youngster. Ask them questions. Acknowledge that they may know more than you and they will be more likely to open up. Trying to be too clever with your use of slang can get in the way of good communication if you are not careful.

• •

5: WHAT ARE THE DIFFERENT WAYS OF TAKING DRUGS?

Mood-altering drugs work by changing the way the brain operates. To do this they need to get into the bloodstream. There are several ways of doing this. Once in the blood-stream the drugs circulate to the brain and the rest of the central nervous system where they begin to have an effect. These effects will usually be depressant or sedative (slow-ing down), stimulant (speeding up) or hallucinogenic (changing perception). The methods of taking drugs are as follows:

Eating/drinking

Here the drug gets into the bloodstream through the wall of the stomach and the small intestine. Examples of taking drugs in this way are drinking alcohol, taking tranquillizers, barbiturates, ecstasy or LSD and eating magic mushrooms.

When drugs are eaten or drunk the effects come on relatively slowly, usually in 10 to 30 minutes.

Smoking/inhaling vapours

This involves breathing in the smoke and fumes produced by burning drugs or the vapours given off by glues, aerosols and other solvents. Smoke or fumes can be breathed in through the mouth and/or the nose. They then pass into the lungs and on into the bloodstream.

Smoking can be done in a cigarette form (called a 'joint' when it contains cannabis) or by burning the drug directly and breathing in the fumes. With heroin this is sometimes called 'chasing the dragon'. Here the heroin is burnt with a match or cigarette lighter through silver foil. The drug turns into a sticky liquid which rolls around the foil and has to be chased by the smoker to keep it burning. The fumes are inhaled.

Glues, solvents, gases and nitrites (poppers) all give off vapours which contain mood-altering drugs. They can be put into bags or poured onto rags and the fumes inhaled. Gases such as butane from cigarette lighter refills are sometimes squirted directly into the mouth. This is particularly dangerous.

Examples of taking drugs by smoking or inhaling include smoking tobacco, cannabis, heroin or crack cocaine, 'sniffing' glues, solvents and gases such as butane, and inhaling nitrites.

When drugs are smoked or inhaled the effects tend to come on quite quickly – usually within a minute or so but sometimes in seconds.

Snorting drugs

Some drugs are snorted up the nose in powder form. The drug is then taken into the bloodstream through the membranes in the nose.

Sometimes quite elaborate methods are used to prepare drugs for snorting. Cocaine can be chopped up into a fine powder with a razor blade. This is usually done on a small mirror to make sure that none of it is lost. (Cocaine is very expensive.) Finally the powder is then snorted up through a straw or sometimes a rolled up banknote.

Examples of drugs which are often snorted are snuff (a form of tobacco), cocaine and amphetamine. Most drugs are not taken in this way.

When drugs are snorted the effects come on within a minute or so.

Injecting drugs

Here a solution of the drug is made up which is then injected using a syringe. Injection can be direct into a vein, into fatty tissue or muscles or sometimes just under the skin. Going straight to the vein causes the fastest and most intense 'hit' of all forms of drug use. Usually the effects are felt within seconds.

Drugs which are often injected are heroin (and other opiate drugs), amphetamines, barbiturates, some tranquillizers, cocaine and steroids.

Injecting is particularly dangerous because of the danger of taking too much in one go (and possibly overdosing) and because of the risk of infection, particularly with HIV (the virus that leads to AIDS) if injecting equipment is shared.

For more information about the dangers associated with the different ways of taking drugs see the following section.

● ●
6: WHAT EFFECTS DO DRUGS HAVE AND WHAT ARE THE REAL DANGERS?

Some people think everyone who takes drugs will end up dead. Some young people seem to think that drug use is one big laugh and not at all dangerous.

The truth is somewhere in between. Drug use can never be 100 per cent safe, but is not always as dangerous as many people think. In order to learn about how drugs affect people and make a careful judgement about the real dangers, it helps to know about the interactions between the *drug*, the *set* and the *setting*. The basic principle is that drug effects are the result of interactions between these three factors. They are not just produced by the drugs themselves.

The *drug* factor is everything connected with the drug and how it is used. The *set* is everything connected with the person who is using the drug. The *setting* is about what the person is doing at the time, where they are, the environment they live in, etc.

The drug

Drugs are not all the same. As already mentioned, there are three main categories: sedative, stimulant and hallucinogenic. The drugs which have a sedative effect (such as alcohol, heroin and tranquillizers) slow down the way the body and brain function. They can have a numbing effect which produces drowsiness if a lot is taken. Other drugs (such as amphetamine, cocaine and ecstasy) have a stimulant effect, giving a rush of energy and making people more alert. A third group of drugs (such as LSD and magic mushrooms and, to a lesser extent, cannabis and ecstasy) have an hallucinogenic effect. This means they tend to alter the way the user feels, sees, hears, tastes or smells. (We describe the effects and risks of different drugs in some detail in Appendix I, 'Facts about drugs', page 127.)

Some drugs are also potentially more dangerous than others. For example, with sedative drugs like alcohol and heroin there is the possibility of taking a fatal overdose. Such drugs can also affect co-ordination, making accidents more likely. Regularly taking sedatives can also lead to physical dependence and withdrawal symptoms, whilst taking other drugs like cannabis cannot.

Stimulant drugs can produce anxiety or panic attacks, particularly if taken in large quantities. They can also be particularly dangerous for people who have heart or blood pressure problems.

Hallucinogenic drugs sometimes produce very disturbing experiences and may lead to erratic or dangerous behaviour by the user, especially if they are already unstable.

And, of course, some drugs are legal to use and others are not. (See 'What does the law say?', page 35.)

The effects and dangers of drug use will also depend on:

How much is taken – The more taken the greater the effect and the greater the danger. Taking too much sedative can lead to a fatal overdose. Taking too much stimulant can lead to over-exhaustion, panic attacks or even, in extreme cases, psychotic behaviour.

How often the drug is taken – The more often a drug is taken, the greater the effect and risks. With some drugs a tolerance can develop such that more needs to be taken in order to keep getting an effect. This can be dangerous if heavy use is followed by a period of non-use. This will lead to a drop in tolerance levels, so if the user then restarts at the same level there is a serious risk of overdose. A number of people have fatally overdosed in this way, particularly after coming out of prison. (Not all drugs produce tolerance. LSD has its own safeguard against tolerance: if it is taken too frequently it just stops working. No matter how much is taken, there will be no effect at all.)

Adulterated drugs – Many illegal drugs, especially in powder or pill form, have all sorts of rubbish and adulterants in them. These can change the effect of the drugs. Sometimes the adulterants are themselves dangerous. It is often difficult to know exactly what is contained in a powder or pill.

Drug mixtures – Combining drugs can produce unpredictable and sometimes dangerous effects. In particular, mixtures of sedative drugs can be very dangerous. Many reported drug overdoses involve mixtures of sedatives. Very often one of the drugs involved is alcohol.

How a drug is taken – The method of use will influence the effect that the drug has. Injecting drugs has a very quick and intense effect. Snorting or inhaling drugs can also have a quick but slightly less intensive effect. Smoking drugs produces a slower, sometimes more mellow effect. The slowest effect of all is obtained by eating or drinking a drug.

Drug dangers also vary with the method used to take them:

Injecting is particularly risky because it is difficult to know how much is being taken. Injection also carries the risk of infection by blood-borne diseases if any injecting equipment is shared. The highest profile recently has been given to HIV, the virus which leads to AIDS, but there are also risks from hepatitis B, a very serious blood-borne disease.

Eating or drinking a drug can be risky if a lot is taken in one go. The effects tend to be slow but once they come on it is too late to do anything about it. Examples are drinking too much alcohol in a short space of time or eating a lump of cannabis. In both cases people can feel suddenly very drunk or stoned and become very disorientated and/or nauseous.

Snorting drugs like amphetamine or cocaine powder up the nose on a regular basis can lead to damage to the nasal membranes, although this risk has probably been exaggerated.

Inhaling solvents such as glues, gases and aerosols can vary in danger. Squirting solvents into a large plastic bag and then placing the bag over the head has led to death by suffocation. Squirting aerosols or butane straight down the throat has led to deaths through freezing of the airways. Squirting onto a rag or small bag then inhaling is not as dangerous.

Smoking a drug is often a less dangerous method of use, although regular use can damage the respiratory system, especially if the drug is smoked with tobacco, as is often the case with cannabis. It has been argued that the most dangerous thing about cannabis is the tobacco it is often smoked with.

INJECTING DRUGS, HIV AND AIDS

Some users who inject drugs share their 'works' with other users. Tiny traces of blood left in the syringe, on the needle or in any of the other equipment used to make injection possible can carry the HIV virus, hepatitis B and other blood-borne infections. Some drug users have passed diseases to each other in this way.

By October 1992 nearly 2,300 people in the UK were known to have become HIV positive in this way. Of these people, 303 had developed AIDS and 177 had died. The UK figures are small compared to some other countries. In New York alone there are an estimated 100,000 drug users who have become HIV positive through sharing 'works'. More than 5,000 of these have already died from AIDS.

The rates of HIV infection amongst injecting drug users vary widely in different parts of the UK. In Liverpool it is less than 1 per cent. In London it is estimated to be 10 per cent and over 25 per cent in Edinburgh. There is a tendency to assume that all of these people are injecting heroin. Many of them will have used heroin, but in some areas other opiate-type drugs are injected as well as tranquillizers and barbiturates. Amphetamine injecting is quite common in some areas and in South Wales, for example, is more prevalent than injecting heroin. Cocaine is also sometimes injected and there has been an increase recently in the number of people who inject steroids.

It doesn't actually matter which drug is being injected from an HIV risk point of view. All sharing of injection equipment is high risk for HIV, no matter which drug is in the syringe.

The best way to reduce the risk of getting HIV in this way is not to use drugs in the first place. For those who do chose to use drugs the message should be: 'Don't inject.' And for those who **will** inject, no matter what we say, the message must be: 'For heaven's sake, don't share injecting equipment.'

Drug injectors should be encouraged to use the needle exchange schemes which have now been established in most parts of the country as part of the battle against AIDS. 'Clean works' are now available free of charge for all drug injectors to help them avoid becoming infected with the viruses or infecting others.

The set

The effects and dangers of drugs are influenced by more than the drugs themselves. Personal factors involving the person who is using the drugs can be just as important as the drugs being used.

The drug experience and the expectations of the user are important. Many young people experimenting with drugs for the first time will be unsure about what to do or what to expect. This ignorance and lack of experience can itself be dangerous.

The effects of drugs and how to get them are learned over time. The first time people use drugs they often find either nothing much happens or they feel sick. This may have happened to you with your first cigarette or drink of alcohol. It is the same for first use of all drugs. Some experimenters decide never to use again but others carry on. Over time they learn how to do it best, what to expect and how to enjoy it most.

The mental or psychological state of the drug user is very important. The mood people are in when they take drugs influences the effects and dangers of drug use. If they are anxious, depressed or unstable, they are more likely to have disturbing experiences when using drugs. They can become more anxious and disorientated, possibly aggressive, 'freak out' and do crazy things or take too much, etc. As a generality, someone who is happy and stable is more likely to use more carefully and not be so badly affected.

Other things about the drug user which may affect their experience of drug use are:

~ Any *physical health problems* like heart disease, high blood pressure, epilepsy, diabetes, asthma or liver problems could make drug use more dangerous. In turn, the drug use could possibly make the health problem worse.

~ The drug user's *energy levels at the time of consuming drugs* can also be important. If they are tired at the time of use then the drug may have a different or more extreme effect than if they are fresh and full of energy.

~ If the user has a low *body weight* the same amount of drugs may affect them more than they would heavier people. Also people who have *eating disorders* like anorexia or bulimia can find that drug use makes it even worse.

~ *Males and females* can experience drugs in different ways. This is both because of their different physical make-up and the different way people view male and female drug use. On average women are of smaller body weight than men, have smaller livers as a proportion of body weight and a greater proportion of body fat. This means that, generally speaking, the same amount of drugs will have a greater effect on a woman than on a man. (Obviously this will not apply with a much larger than average woman or a much smaller than average man.)

The effects and risks of drug use are also influenced by attitudes towards men and women taking drugs. Women are often seen as doubly bad if they take drugs: they are bad for taking drugs and, if they are mothers, their drug use is seen as a betrayal of this role. We cannot understand why it is that male drug users who are parents are not seen in the same way. It seems that sexism can also affect the experience of drug use and drug risks.

This also spills over to the way *pregnant women* who use drugs are viewed. Many drugs – including alcohol and nicotine – can cross the placenta and adversely affect an unborn child. This is especially the case with heavy, regular drug use during pregnancy. Possible effects include increased risk of miscarriage, low birth weight, developmental problems and foetal distress. These will vary from drug to drug and can also be influenced by many other things including diet, housing conditions, levels of stress and support and medical help. Drug use needs to be kept in perspective. The media have used sensationalized stories of 'newborn heroin addicts' or 'crack babies' and the extent to which drug use can affect an unborn child has often been exaggerated. This does not help pregnant users feel positive about themselves or being mothers or encourage them to seek medical help.

The setting

Where drugs are used can affect the risks. Some youngsters take drugs in out-of-the-way places which are particularly dangerous – on canal banks, near motorways, in derelict buildings, etc. Accidents are much more likely in these places, especially if the user is intoxicated. Also, if anything does go wrong, it is unlikely help will be at hand or that an ambulance could easily be called.

Even if the setting is not in itself inherently dangerous there may be other types of risks associated with the place of use. Thus using or taking drugs into school has led to substantial numbers of young people being expelled, with drastic effects on their future careers.

What people are doing whilst they are using drugs can be an extra risk. Driving a car, riding a bicycle or operating machinery whilst on drugs will greatly increase the risk of accidents. Also, drug use can lower inhibitions, which may lead to a greater likelihood of getting into sexual situations whilst under the influence. Avoiding intercourse or practising safer sex – i.e. by using condoms – will be much more difficult if the person concerned is intoxicated. The risks of unwanted pregnancy, HIV and other sexually transmitted diseases are probably increased if young people have sex whilst high on alcohol or drugs. A recent survey in Liverpool suggested that as many as a third of all sexual encounters by young people under 20 took place whilst under the influence. (For more about the interaction between drug use and sex, see 'What about drugs, sex and AIDS?', page 48.)

Another recently highlighted danger is that of young people over-exerting themselves when using ecstasy. Ecstasy gives a buzz of energy and is often used in clubs whilst dancing non-stop for long periods. Sometimes young people dance for hours without a break in hot, crowded environments, thereby running the risk of becoming dehydrated and getting heat exhaustion. This can be very dangerous and has led to a small number of deaths. 'Chillin' out' – having a break from dancing, cooling off and drinking plenty of water or fruit juice (not alcohol as it further dehydrates the user) – reduces these risks.

To understand fully how drugs affect young people and what the real risks and dangers are you will need to think about the *drug*, *set* and *setting*. To do this you will have to be able to communicate openly and honestly with your youngster – something we focus on in Part II of this book.

●●●●●●●●●●●●●●●●●●●●●●●●●●●●●●●●●●●●●●

7: WHAT DOES THE LAW SAY?

The laws covering the use of controlled ('illegal') drugs, as well as those covering 'legal' drugs like alcohol and cigarettes, are complicated. It might help to start by saying what we mean by controlled drugs.

Controlled drugs

The main law covering the use of drugs in the UK is the *Misuse of Drugs Act*. This law controls the possession, supply and production of street drugs like heroin, cocaine and crack, cannabis, amphetamine, ecstasy and LSD. Drugs can also be controlled by the *Medicines Act*, which affects a wider range of drugs but is aimed more at the manufacture and supply of medicines than the street use of drugs. Drugs controlled by either of these two laws are known as 'controlled drugs'.

There are other laws covering the sale of legal drugs such as alcohol, tobacco and some substances such as solvents, as well as laws covering drunken driving and driving whilst under the influence of drink or drugs. This next section will concentrate mainly on the Misuse of Drugs Act. If you need more detailed information on other laws, have a look at some of the books recommended in Appendix II of this book, page 165.

Before you look through our notes on drug laws, test how much you already know. Have a go at the following quiz.

DRUG LAWS QUIZ

Are these people breaking the law?
Answer yes or no.

1. Two 15 year olds go into a pub by themselves.

2. A mother finds some ecstasy tablets in her daughter's bedroom. According to the father, the law says they have to call the police and hand over the drugs. The mother decides to flush the tablets down the toilet and not tell anyone.

3. A 17 year old grows cannabis plants in the greenhouse at home.

4. A mother has valium on prescription. She gives a couple to her son on the morning of his driving test as he is so nervous.

5. A nine year old sniffs from aerosols in a local park.

6. Three 16 year olds go into a field and pick and eat magic mushrooms.

7. A shopkeeper sells cigarettes to a 12 year old.

8. An 18 year old has a number of syringes.

9. Someone offers to get some heroin for a friend but none is available.

10. A parent drinks three pints of lager in quick succession, hops in their car and drives home.

Answers on page 57.

THE MISUSE OF DRUGS ACT (MDA)

This law makes the possession, supply, cultivation and manufacture of certain drugs illegal. The drugs it controls are divided into three classes: A, B and C. This law acts as if the Class A drugs are the most dangerous, Class B next most dangerous and Class C least dangerous.

The penalties are graded so that the highest penalties are given for offences involving the Class A drugs. A short list of the best known drugs in each class is given below. (For full lists you will need to see a copy of the Act, which

you can get from your local branch of HMSO (Her
Majesty's Stationery Office). Look your nearest one up in
your telephone book. Every major city has one.)

Class A drugs include: Cocaine, crack, ecstasy, heroin,
LSD, methadone, morphine, PCP (phencyclidine),
processed magic mushrooms and any Class B drug
which is prepared for injection.

Class B drugs include: Amphetamines, barbiturates,
cannabis, codeine, dihydrocodeine pain-killers
(DF 118).

Class C drugs include: Tranquillizers such as valium
and some minor amphetamine-type drugs.

There is a range of offences under the Act, covering:

~ Possession.

~ Possession with intent to supply.

~ Supply or attempting to supply.

~ Production, cultivation or manufacture.

~ Import and export.

~ Allowing premises to be used for consumption (of
some controlled drugs), supply, cultivation,
manufacture, etc.

The penalties depend on the class of the drug concerned.
The maximum penalties are:

	POSSESSION	SUPPLY
Class A	7 years + fine	Life imprisonment + a fine
Class B	5 years + fine	14 years + a fine
Class C	2 years + fine	5 years + a fine

These severe penalties can only be imposed by the Crown Court with a judge and jury. The magistrates' courts have maximum sentences of six months imprisonment and a fine of no more than £2,000.

All of these sentences will depend on the individual case. The figures given above are maximums. In practice a first offence of possession, particularly of a Class B drug like cannabis, might only receive a fine or even a police caution. Despite the increased use of cautions by the police for possession offences there are almost 20,000 convictions a year in the UK for possession of cannabis.

The law is complicated by the fact that some drugs can legally be in someone's possession if they have a prescription for them. Methadone, morphine, heroin and all the Class B drugs recorded above except cannabis can all be legally prescribed in this way.

THE MEDICINES ACT

The 1968 Medicines Act governs the manufacture and supply of medicines and its enforcement rarely affects the public. It can, however, be used to prosecute people for selling drugs like steroids. Penalties are less severe than under the Misuse of Drugs Act.

Other drugs

ALCOHOL

Despite being the world's second biggest killer drug (after tobacco) alcohol is not controlled under the Misuse of Drugs Act.

The law allows a 14 year old to go into licensed premises such as a pub, but not to drink alcohol. A 16 year old can legally buy and consume beer, port, cider or perry (but not spirits) if they are also having a meal in an area set aside for that purpose. It is not illegal for under 18s to drink alcohol away from licensed premises unless they are under 5 years of age. It is an offence for a licensed vendor to knowingly sell alcohol to an under 18 year old. A few areas have brought in controls on the consumption of alcohol in certain public places, but this is still rare.

KETAMINE

Ketamine has recently found its way on to the drug scene in a limited way. It is not yet controlled under the Misuse of Drugs Act, although it has been suggested for inclusion. It is controlled under the Medicines Act, so although it is not illegal to possess or use the drug it is illegal to sell or supply it to someone else.

MAGIC MUSHROOMS

These are not controlled in themselves under the Misuse of Drugs Act, but they do contain a chemical (psilocin) which is a Class A drug. This means that in their raw state they are not controlled but if prepared in any way – by drying them out, cooking with them or making them into a tea – they are viewed as preparations of the controlled drug and become Class A.

NITRITES (POPPERS/LIQUID GOLD)

There are no legal controls over these drugs. They are widely available in joke and sex shops and in clubs, although recently there has been some evidence of police forces suggesting to vendors that they should be treated in a similar way to solvents (see below) and that they should not be sold to under 18s.

OVER THE COUNTER (OTC) MEDICINES

There is a wide range of over the counter medicines which can be brought from a chemist without a prescription and used for their intoxicating effect. They include cough medicines which contain opiates and other medicines which can have sedative, stimulant or hallucinogenic properties.

SOLVENTS, GLUES AND GASES
These are not controlled under the Misuse of Drugs Act. In England and Wales it is an offence for a shopkeeper to sell such substances to an under 18 year old if they know they are likely to be used for intoxicating purposes. There is also the possibility that young people under the influence might be charged with public order offences if they are making a nuisance of themselves.

STEROIDS
These are controlled under the Medicines Act. They can only legally be sold by a pharmacist and only obtained on prescription from a doctor. This means that it is illegal to supply them to another person but not illegal to be the one supplied. There is the chance that they might be brought under control of the Misuse of Drugs Act in the future.

TOBACCO
It is not illegal to possess or use tobacco or supply it to another person at no charge. It is only illegal for a vendor to knowingly sell tobacco products to an under 16. It is not illegal for an under 16 to smoke cigarettes.

TRANQUILLIZERS
These are Class C drugs under the Misuse of Drugs Act but the possession offence does not apply if the drugs are in the form of a medicine. It is thus not an offence to possess them or use them in their medicinal/tablet form but it is still an offence to supply them to another person. This applies whether or not any money changes hands.

8: WHAT DO DIFFERENT DRUGS LOOK LIKE?

Imagine that you have come across a powder, some pills or a strange looking substance in your youngster's bedroom. What is it? Is it a drug and if so which? Understandably a lot of parents want to know what different drugs look like. The problem is that it's not that simple.

Take cannabis, for example. Cannabis comes from a plant – *Cannabis sativa*. The plant can be bushy and/or very tall – three to four feet in the UK, up to ten feet high in a very hot country. Yet in the UK you are unlikely to see a cannabis plant growing. Most often you will see cannabis as a block of resin. This has been scraped from the leaves of the plant and made into a block. It can vary in colour from light golden or greeny brown to very dark brown or black. It can feel light, dry and crumbly or heavy, oily and very hard. Both texture and colour can vary between these extremes – on the one hand, imagine a chicken or stock cube but a little harder; on the other, a piece of French chalk but much darker, maybe almost black.

In addition to the resin you might come across herbal cannabis. This is the cannabis leaves themselves, dried out and ready to smoke. The colour and texture of the leaves will vary depending upon where they have been grown. Imported herbal cannabis will be different in texture and colour from home grown. Even experienced users have occasionally been caught out buying dried everyday herbs and grasses believing them to be cannabis.

Finally, you might come across cannabis oil. This is extracted from the resin and is the strongest concentration of cannabis found in the UK. It is very dark and oily, looking a bit like treacle.

Cannabis has a very distinctive smell which once you

have smelled it you are unlikely to forget. But if you have not smelled it yet – well, smells are very difficult to describe. Try and describe the smell of garlic to someone who doesn't know what it is. It's almost impossible – garlic smells like ... garlic, and that's all there is to it. Cannabis is the same. It smells like ... cannabis.

Complicated isn't it? And cannabis is much easier for a novice to recognize than many other drugs.

Powders

Some drugs, such as amphetamine, cocaine and heroin, come in powder form. They can vary in colour depending on where, when and how they have been processed. All of the 'laboratories' making these drugs are highly illegal and none are subject to quality control. Each batch may be different from the last. All sorts of rubbish can creep in or get mixed in to add to the volume.

The colour and consistency will vary enormously. Heroin, for example, can be white, grey, cream coloured, brownish and all shades in between. Even regular users get ripped off sometimes buying powdered milk or laxatives dressed up to look like heroin or cocaine. There are also medicines and many household products which are these colours.

Tablets

Identifying drugs is even harder when they are in tablet form. There are literally thousands of different medicines that come in this form and this makes it difficult to distinguish drugs such as amphetamines, ecstasy, tranquillizers or steroids.

LSD

LSD can come in a variety of forms. Sometimes it is in the form of impregnated squares of blotting paper. Some of these are overprinted to look like the transfers you see young children playing with. In some areas there have been drug scares when parents have thought local children playing with transfers might be using LSD. It has not been LSD and it is very unlikely that young children would come into contact with it. However, the confusion arose because the everyday transfers *looked* like LSD squares. Many of the street names for the drug are derived from the printed picture or appearance – e.g. strawberries, penguins, rainbows, Gorbachovs, ferns, etc.

LSD can also be dripped onto sugar cubes or processed with sugar into mini tablets. These are home made and come in all sorts of shapes – stars, diamonds, etc.

Drug paraphernalia

These are the things drug users will sometimes have about them to help them use drugs. Take great care with these, as most of them have very legitimate uses that have nothing to do with drugs.

Cannabis is usually smoked. In order to make up cannabis cigarettes ('joints') there will be cigarette papers and usually small rolled up tubes of cardboard for the filter tip or 'roach'. Sometimes mini pipes are used or more elaborate hubble bubble pipes to draw the smoke through water, cooling it. The cannabis will sometimes be supplied in little self-sealing plastic bags or in twists of silver foil or cling film.

Smoking powdered drugs like heroin is often done by 'chasing the dragon'. This involves heating the powder up to the point at which it vaporizes or gives off smoke which is then drawn up into the mouth or nose through a straw or rolled up paper tube. The powder will be put onto tinfoil or perhaps a metal spoon so that a match or cigarette lighter can be used from below. These items may be found in a burnt or discoloured state.

Drugs prepared for injection must be made into a solution which will go through a syringe. The paraphernalia can include needles and syringes, water, lemon juice, citric acid, cigarette filter tips or pieces of tampon (to trap any chalk from crushed tablets in solution), a rubber tube or strap to act as tourniquet when preparing the veins to receive the needle and metal bottle tops, spoons or similar to act as 'cooker' for the water.

Other items associated with drug use include:

~ foil containers or cup shapes made from silver foil
~ metal tins
~ pill boxes
~ plastic, cellophane or metal foil wrappers
~ small plastic or glass phials or bottles
~ twists of paper
~ straws
~ sugar lumps
~ syringes and needles
~ spent matches
~ plastic bags with traces of glue
~ butane gas cylinders
~ stamps, stickers, transfers
~ shredded or home-made cigarettes
~ torn cigarette packets or pieces of card

WARNING

Given the everyday objects listed above and how difficult it can be to recognize different drugs for sure, we cannot finish this part of the book without stressing *if in doubt ask your youngsters, but do it in a low key way.*

For advice on what to actually do if you find something you think is suspicious see Part III, 'Coping in a crisis', page 107.

• •

9: HOW CAN YOU TELL IF YOUR YOUNGSTER IS USING DRUGS?

As a parent you will want to know if your youngster is using drugs. What should you be looking out for? One way would to find drugs or drug paraphernalia as described above. However, there are also lists of signs and symptoms that have been put together to try to help parents know what changes in behaviour or appearance to look out for in their youngsters. Could you therefore look through these lists, keep an eye on your youngsters and spot the tell-tale signs of drug use? Unfortunately, it is not always that easy.

Signs and symptoms

Below is an extract from *Drug Misuse and the Young: A Guide for the Education Service*, a pamphlet published by the Department for Education in 1992 (reproduced with the permission of the Controller of Her Majesty's Stationery Office). It aims to help teachers to recognize the signs of drug use in young people.

Warning signs in individuals

~ Decline in performance in school work or youth club activities.

~ Changes in attendance and being unwilling to take part in school or youth club group activities.

~ Unusual outbreaks of temper, marked swings of moods, restlessness or irritability.

~ Reports from parents that more time is being spent away from home, possibly with new friends or with friends in older age groups.

~ Excessive spending or borrowing of money.

~ Stealing money or goods.

~ Excessive tiredness without obvious cause.

~ No interest in physical appearance.

~ Sores or rashes, especially on the mouth or nose.

~ Lack of appetite.

~ Heavy use of scents, colognes etc. to disguise the smell of drugs.

~ Wearing sunglasses at inappropriate times (to hide dilated or constricted pupils).

Warning signs in groups

~ Regular absence on certain days (e.g. the day young people receive state benefits).

~ Keeping at a distance from other pupils, students or youth club members, away from supervision points (e.g. groups who frequently gather near the gate of a school playground or sports field)

~ Being the subject of rumours about drug taking.

~ Talking to strangers on or near the premises.

~ Stealing which appears to be the work of several individuals rather than one person (e.g. perhaps to shoplift solvents).

~ Use of drug takers' slang.

~ Exchanging money or other subjects in unusual circumstances.

~ Associating briefly with one person who is much older and not normally part of the peer group.

The problem is that many of the listed signs and symptoms are normal aspects of adolescent behaviour. All of them could be due to things other than drug use.

Most of the time using a drug does not result in clear signs and symptoms unless you happen to be with the user whilst they are actually intoxicated. Think about alcohol for a moment. You cannot tell if someone uses alcohol just by looking at them. Perhaps you could smell alcohol on their breath if they had just had a drink. Maybe if they were a really heavy drinker they might have a red face. But most of the time you wouldn't be able to tell. It's just the same with other drugs. The lists of signs and symptoms usually apply to the very heavy and chaotic users. These are only a small minority. Most young people use drugs occasionally and do not fall into this category.

Drug effects are complex. The same drug can produce different effects on different people. The same drug can even produce different effects on the same person at different times depending on their mood, as explained earlier (see page 31). So predicting drug use by trying to spot its effects can be an unreliable business. What if you get it wrong? Young people will resent being accused of things they have not done. The 'signs' may be nothing more than unconfirmed rumours and your imagination.

There are parallels here with the previous section on drug recognition, and in both cases there is no substitute for *talking and listening to your youngsters*. If you think they are behaving oddly and are worried about the possibility of drug use, say so. Tell them about your concerns. Listen carefully to what they have to say. The key is communication with your youngster (see Part II for ideas on how to achieve good communication). Parents and youngsters talking can break through the mystique of drug use. Lists of signs and symptoms have only a very small value in helping that communication process.

• •

10: WHAT ABOUT DRUGS, SEX AND AIDS?

N.B. This part is about sex and drugs. For information about the risks of AIDS from injecting drugs, see 'What effects do drugs have and what are the real dangers?', page 26.

Sex 'n' drugs 'n' rock 'n' roll. That was what the 1960s were supposed to be about. In the 1990s, electronic dance music has taken over from rock 'n' roll but the sex and drugs are still there.

Alcohol is the drug most commonly used to overcome inhibitions, to help people relax and often to help develop so-called 'Dutch courage'. Having loosened up in the bar, young people will loosen up on the dance floor and hope to loosen up later in bed or in the back seat of someone's car. One problem arising from this is that safer sex often goes out of the window once a few drinks are taken. It is difficult to be in control, avoid unprotected intercourse or to use

condoms if you are out of your head. And of course for
many that's not just the result of alcohol. Other drugs and
sex often go together.

A recent survey in Liverpool showed that about 30 per
cent of all the young people asked – over 1,000 – reported
having sex under the influence of drink or drugs. Of these
about a third said that it was sex that would not have taken
place if they had not been intoxicated. Whenever sexual
intercourse takes place there are risks both of unwanted
pregnancy and of sexually transmitted diseases such as
HIV/AIDS and hepatitis as well as diseases like syphilis,
gonorrhoea and chlamydia.

Because there are so many myths about drugs and sex it
is worth making a few notes on what is known:

amphetamines These are widely used as a 'dance
   drug' by young people. They have been claimed to
   prevent premature ejaculation and prolong sexual
   interest in both males and females but they can tend
   to reduce the likelihood of either achieving an
   orgasm. Sometimes it is said that prolonged use of
   amphetamine will reduce the size of a man's penis.
   Not perhaps the most attractive feature of the drug!

barbiturates See under 'heroin'.

caffeine and tobacco These popular legal drugs have
   their part to play in the game of sex, although it is
   more in the rituals before and after than in the act
   itself. The post-coital cigarette is not as popular as it
   once was and the idea of making love to someone
   who has a fag in their mouth must be one of life's
   great turn-offs. Caffeine puts in appearance at an
   earlier stage in the mating game, as in, 'Are you
   coming back for a coffee or something?'

cannabis Using cannabis produces a mellowing effect which can enhance sexual pleasure. The ways in which perception is changed by the drug can also increase the intensity of sexual pleasure if the users learn to interpret the effects that way. Taking larger doses of cannabis can produce nausea, diarrhoea or vomiting, which will not help sexual attractiveness! Cannabis use can also result in short-term memory loss, making remembering to practise safer sex more difficult.

cocaine Not too much is known about sex and cocaine, although some male and female users have been known to put a bit on their genitals to attempt to enhance and prolong sexual pleasure.

ecstasy This is also a dance drug and has been described as 'the love drug' or sometimes 'the hug drug'. This is because users often report that they lose any feelings of anger or hostility and are taken over by serene feelings of well-being and affection. The experience tends to enhance feelings of sexual pleasure rather than increase libido. As with amphetamines, it may also inhibit orgasm and male erection. There is debate about whether its use will increase the risk of unsafe sex or decrease it.

heroin, the opiates, barbiturates, tranquillizers, glue and solvents These drugs are all sedatives and tend to reduce interest in sex. They will probably lead to an individual going more into themselves than into interaction with others. There have been claims that heavy use of sedatives by women makes them more vulnerable to sexual abuse and exploitation.

There is also clear evidence of high levels of

sedative use amongst prostitutes, although the cause-effect relationship is not clear. Are the prostitutes selling themselves to raise money for drugs or using drugs to block out the unpleasantness of prostitution? Perhaps it is a bit of both in some sort of interaction.

LSD In the 1990s LSD has made a comeback as another dance drug. Its effects are unpredictable. Sometimes an intense, almost religious, ecstatic experience is reported. In some individuals LSD use will lower sexual interest as the user goes off into their own inner world. In others the loss of inhibitions that accompanies the drug use will enhance sexual pleasure. Magic mushrooms have similar effects to LSD, although milder.

magic mushrooms See under 'LSD'.

nitrites Amyl and butyl nitrite (liquid gold) have a history of being used in clubs and pubs, particularly by gay men, to increase sexual desire and pleasure, often at the moment of orgasm. They certainly relax the muscles around the anus, making anal sex easier. More recently they have come into common use amongst young people as aphrodisiacs.

solvents See under 'heroin'.

steroids These are a group of hormones which occur naturally in the body and are involved in the working of the reproductive organs. The main male hormone is testosterone. Because steroids interact with the body's own hormones they can have complex effects on sexual functioning when taken as external drugs.

In men the body lowers its own production of testosterone, lowering sperm count. Sex drive may be increased at first, but with increased use of steroids will be diminished. There are many reports of aggression and sexual violence by men using large amounts of steroids. There are also reports of 'testicular atrophy' (shrinking of genitals) amongst regular male users.

Women using steroids may experience increased sex drive, irregular periods and an enlarged clitoris. There are also reports of women decreasing in breast size and developing facial hair and sometimes a deepening of the voice. These effects seem to be irreversible.

tranquillizers See under 'heroin'.

tobacco See under 'caffeine'.

CONCLUSION

What can parents do about drugs and sex? It will certainly help to brief yourself about the ways in which sex and drugs might interact. In addition to concerns about drug use, many parents will also be concerned about the risks of sex at too early an age, sexually transmitted diseases and unwanted pregnancy. By being prepared to discuss these matters openly with your children you will be in the best position to help them to reduce these risks.

• •

11: WHAT KIND OF HELP IS AVAILABLE?

There are different kinds of help available for people who have problems with drugs or need advice and information. 'Know where and how to get help in your area', page 96, explains what you need to do to get help, and further resources are listed in Appendix II, page 165. Below we briefly describe the different types of help that are available across the UK. The best way to find out about drug services in your area is to ring 0800 66 55 44. This is a free telephone health information service now operating in every part of the UK. They should have details of all the local health services, including those for people with drug problems.

Family doctors

The family doctor or GP is the cornerstone of health services in the UK. GPs should be able to offer you help and advice on drug problems as on other family health issues. They can give you or your youngster advice, sometimes prescribe substitute drugs and certainly should have information on local specialist services.

Sadly, however, some family doctors are simply not up to scratch when it comes to dealing with drug issues. They may have been trained before drug problems became widespread in the UK and even today GP training does not adequately deal with how to work with drug users. Despite this, many GPs have made the effort to inform themselves and can sometimes provide an excellent service. Do not be too surprised though if your GP cannot cope well with drug use. If you wish, you can always change your GP or, if you are satisfied with their performance in other respects, you might want to go elsewhere for drug advice and support. Fortunately there are a range of other services available.

Drug advice and counselling services

The names of these services vary. In some areas they are called Community Drug Teams or Drug Advice Services, but often they have a name which is specific to the area they operate in. They give information and advice and offer counselling to drug users and/or their parents. They usually offer advice over the phone as well as seeing people by appointment.

Services offered vary from area to area:

~ Some services operate drop in services whilst others are only by appointment.

~ Some services meet people only at the project base whilst others will come out to meet clients in their homes or in the community.

~ Some services have their own doctors who can prescribe substitute drugs and offer syringe and needle exchange facilities.

~ Some services work with self-help groups and rehabilitation centres.

These services are usually confidential – no one outside the service will know you or your youngster has been in contact.

Until recently few such organizations worked with young people under the age of 16, usually focusing on the 18-plus age range, especially those who inject drugs like heroin. This is gradually changing and whilst some still only see under 16s with parental consent, many are now offering services to them without parental consent if necessary.

Non-specialist young people's advice and counselling services

These types of services exist in some areas. They do not specialize in drugs but they do specialize in working with young people. Local colleges, youth clubs or youth projects sometimes offer similar confidential services for young people.

Hospital-based drug services

These are usually for people who are heavy, long-term drug users, particularly injecting heroin users. Some offer stable 'maintenance' prescribing. This aims to stabilize the user on steady doses of a clean alternative to street heroin, usually the opioid drug methadone. Some services will steadily reduce the prescription to ease people off the drug altogether. This service can also be offered by GPs. A few hospital-based drug services prescribe other drugs.

Treatments do vary between different clinics. These services usually require a letter of referral from a GP, social worker, probation officer or local drug service. Hospital beds may be available if needed, but there is often a waiting list.

Residential rehabilitation centres

These are for people with longer term drug problems, usually involving dependency. Users live in them for up to a year in an attempt to kick the habit. If there is no such facility in your area local users may be able to go to centres elsewhere in the country. Part of the costs can be met through benefits, although recent changes in Community Care arrangements have produced funding problems for these services. Information about them can be obtained through your local drugs advice service (see above).

Self-help groups for drug users, parents and families

These exist in many areas. Your local drugs advice service should be able to tell you what is available. You can also contact the health information services line on 0800 66 55 44 or one of the following national organizations:

ADFAM – The national charity for families and friends
of drug users. Runs a national helpline – tel. 071–638
3700 – and provides training courses, including for
parents.

Families Anonymous – are involved in support
groups for parents and families of drug users in
different parts of the country. Tel. 071–498 4680.

Narcotics Anonymous – this is a network of self-help
groups for drug users based on the Alcoholics
Anonymous approach. Tel. 071–498 9005.

Release run a 24-hour national helpline specially for
people who have been arrested for a drug offence.
They also give legal advice to parents. They can be
contacted on 071–603 8654.

Needle/syringe exchange schemes

These are for injecting drug users. They aim to ensure that
drug injectors do not have to share injecting equipment.
This should limit the spread of HIV and AIDS. Some
exchange schemes are based within drug advice projects
but others operate from chemist shops or hospitals.
Some exchange schemes also include outreach workers
who meet users in their homes or on the streets. They are
confidential services. Users do not have to give their name.
As well as clean injecting equipment they also offer advice,
information and access to health services.

In conclusion

There are now helping services of various kinds available
in different parts of the country. Do find out what is available in your locality (see 'Finding out more about drug use

in your area', page 7) and do not feel shy about approaching
services if you feel you need them.

DRUG LAWS QUIZ ANSWERS

From page 36.

1. **No**. Young people over 14 are allowed into a pub by
themselves so long as they do not buy or consume alcohol.

2. **No**. If you find illegal drugs you do not have to inform the
police. You can destroy them yourself. But don't hang on to
them or you will be at risk of prosecution for possession of
controlled drugs.

3. **Yes**. Growing cannabis plants is an offence. Also, if the
parents know it is happening on their premises and do not
try to stop it, they could themselves be prosecuted for
allowing their premises to be used for the production of
controlled drugs.

4. **Yes**. She is breaking the law but the son is not. The supply
of tranquillizers to another person is illegal under both the
Medicines and Misuse of Drugs Acts but it is not illegal to
use them, with or without a prescription.

5. **No**. It is not illegal to use aerosols, glues or other solvents,
at any age. It is only illegal to sell or supply solvents to an
under 18 knowing that they will use them for intoxication.
However, there have been cases of young people being
charged with public order offences such as 'Behaviour likely
to cause a breach of the peace' after becoming high on
glues/solvents in public places.

6. **No**. Magic mushrooms are not illegal to use raw. They are
only illegal to use if processed, made into a tea, cooked
with, etc. In such a case they are viewed as a controlled
drug under the Misuse of Drugs Act.

7. **Yes**. The 12 year old is not breaking the law but the
shopkeeper is. It is not illegal to buy or use cigarettes at any
age but it is illegal for a shopkeeper to knowingly sell them
to an under 16 year old.

8. **No**. It is not illegal to possess or use injecting equipment. It

depends what drugs are injected. If it is tranquillizers the
user is not breaking the law. They might also inject insulin –
they might be diabetic. Even if they are injecting heroin it is
not the use itself which is illegal, but the possession of
heroin, which is controlled under the Misuse of Drugs Act.

9. **Yes**. The person who offered to get the heroin could be
prosecuted with conspiring to supply a controlled drug.

10. **Yes (probably)**. The legal limit for drink driving is about two
and a half pints for most men and slightly less for most
women.

How did you do? If you got less than six right you might want to do
some more research. Have a look through the notes on the Misuse
of Drugs Act on pages 36–7 and maybe look up few of the books
recommended in Appendix II, page 165.

Part II

●●●●●●●●●●●●●●●●●●●●●●●●●●●●●●●●●●●

What every parent can
do: Be prepared

●●●●●●●●●●●●●●●●●●●●●●●●●●●●●●●●●●●

1: BE INFORMED – LEARN FACTS NOT MYTHS

'All they say is "Don't do it" or "It'll kill you." We still do it. They don't know what they're talking about.'
— 15 year old

In order to be prepared, you must first be informed. You don't have to know everything about drugs, but you do need to avoid the many myths and half-truths which surround drug use. This can be difficult because the harm from drug use is often overstated. Sometimes an extreme example is presented as though it is what normally happens every time. Drug issues are often presented on television and in the newspapers in an exaggerated and sensationalized way. Drug users in films and novels are usually sleazy, low-life characters. The vast majority of drug use is totally unlike these stereotypes. In view of this it can be difficult to keep illicit drug use in its proper perspective.

It may help to revise the reasons why young people use drugs. Have a look at the exercise below and see if it helps to sharpen up your understanding.

REASONS WHY YOUNG PEOPLE USE DRUGS

Look through the list below of reasons why someone might use drugs.

1. Drugs are freely **available**.
2. **Everyone** does it.
3. It's the **fashion**.
4. It's **fun**.
5. It makes you feel **good**.
6. It's **exciting**.

7. **Pressure** from other young people.
8. It's a **protest** against society and adults.
9. Out of **boredom**.
10. To try to **block out feelings** of emotional pain or inadequacy.

Now answer the questions which follow. Write down the key words you think fit best on a piece of paper.

1. Which of the reasons best explains why:

   a) A 14 year old might experiment with sniffing butane gas with their friends.

   b) A 16 year old locks themselves in their bedroom all day and sniffs three canisters of butane gas.

   c) A 17 year old smokes cannabis with their friends at weekends when it is available.

   d) A 16 year old takes ecstasy every weekend and goes to all night raves with a crowd who also use.

   e) An 18 year old chain-smokes and drinks at least six pints of lager a day with their mates.

   f) A 16 year old has been prescribed tranquillizers by their doctor after the death of their mother.

2. Which of the reasons best explain your use of drugs (legal and illegal) when you were young?

3. Which of the reasons might apply to your youngster(s) today?

Now ask your youngster to go through the questions with you and discuss your answers with them.

Now have a go at the quiz that follows. It will help you further to sift some of the drug myths from the reality.

DRUG MYTHS QUIZ

Work out whether each of the statements below is true or a myth.

Answer true or false:

1. All drug use is dangerous.
2. Illegal drugs are more dangerous than the legal ones.
3. More people die through use of alcohol each year than through heroin.
4. Once they start on cannabis they go on to heroin.
5. Most people who take drugs come to no serious harm.
6. One try of heroin, cocaine or crack and you are 'hooked' for life.
7. Most drug users commit crime to get the money to buy drugs.
8. Only a small number of youngsters try illegal drugs.
9. It is often very difficult to spot if someone is using drugs.
10. Most young people get their drugs from their friends.
11. All illegal drugs come into this country from abroad.
12. Illegal drugs are not always that expensive.
13. Young people take drugs because they mix with the wrong sort.
14. I take drugs.
15. If young people knew how dangerous drugs were they wouldn't use them.

Answers on page 103.

Some other things you can do are:

1. Try the quiz with your partner, a friend and/or your youngster.
2. Think about some of the other myths that surround drug use. What are they and why do people believe

them? Discuss this with your partner, a friend
and/or your youngster. Ask your youngster what
drug myths they think parents often believe.

3. Look at the way television, magazines and
newspapers report on drug issues. What myths and
stereotypes do they use?

4. Learn more by reading books (see Appendix II,
'Where to find out more', page 165) or going on local
education workshops or courses.

*'I know it's true that most young people use drugs
without getting into harm. I know it but still find it
difficult to bring myself to believe it.'* – Parent

*'I have realized that I do know quite a lot about drugs.
In the past I was so anxious about it that I couldn't
think sensibly or clearly – I sort of forgot what I
already knew.'* – Parent

• •

2: THINK ABOUT YOUR OWN USE OF DRUGS

*'I booze regularly, smoke fags and drink gallons of
coffee. When I was young I tried speed and smoked
cannabis. But basically I don't believe in drugs.'* – Parent

One interesting definition of drugs is: 'Drugs are something
other people do.' In fact we often do not see our own drug
use as being drug use at all. But almost all of us take, or
have taken, drugs of one sort or another. Even those of us
who are teetotal, don't smoke, never use aspirin or other
medicines and don't drink tea, coffee or soft drinks have

probably used some of them at some time in the past.

Think about your own drug use both now and in the past. What has it been like? How does it influence your attitudes towards young people's drug use today? What sort of messages does your own use of drugs (past and present) give to your own youngster(s)?

In order to help you do this, try the following exercise.

YOUR OWN DRUG USE

Look at the list of drugs below. Then answer the questions. Finally, talk through your answers with your partner or a friend.

The drugs

alcohol	magic mushrooms
amphetamine	poppers (nitrites)
aspirin/codeine	sleeping pills
barbiturates	solvents
cannabis	(glue/gas/aerosols, etc.)
cocaine/crack	steroids
ecstasy	tea, coffee (caffeine)
heroin (or other opiate drugs)	tobacco
LSD	tranquillizers

The questions

1. Which drugs have you ever used?
2. Which ones did you try when you were young?
3. Why did you try them?
4. Did you enjoy your use of drugs when you were young? If so, in what ways?
5. Which drugs have you used in the past year?

6. Why do you use them?

7. Overall, has your use of drugs been a good or bad experience?

8. What does this tell you about:

a) you as a youngster?

b) your life now?

c) how drug use might change as people get older?

d) young people's use of drugs?

e) the example you set for your youngster?

Drug careers

We all have *drug careers*. At different stages of our lives our drug use changes. At one time we might be using almost no drugs at all. At another time we might be experimenting with lots of different drugs. At yet another time we might be using just one or two drugs but using them regularly. It depends on what is going on in our lives at the time.

Try plotting a *Drug Career Graph* for yourself like the one overleaf. Choose one or two drugs you have used over the years. Alcohol is often a good one to start with.

Note on the graph how your use of the drug has changed over the years. Then look at the graph and think about what was going on in your life at these different times.

What does it tell you about your drug use? What lessons might there be about young people's drug use? Discuss your drug career with a partner or friend and ask them about their drug career.

Explaining your drug use to your youngster

'My drug use? You're joking? I thought this was about what my son has been up to.' — Parent

Drug Career Graph

VERY HEAVY,
EVERY DAY USE

· ·

MODERATE,
REGULAR USE

· ·

MODERATE,
OCCASIONAL USE

· ·

NO USE
AT ALL

AGE   5   15   25   35   45   65   75

Few parents explain to their youngsters just what they themselves got up to when they were young. Perhaps we are worried they will make the same mistakes that we did, that we will put ideas into their heads or that it will sound as though we are saying they can do the same.

Despite this it is a good idea to let them know that we were young once. They might even learn something useful from our experiences – both good and bad. Try talking to your youngster about your drug use when you were young and your drug use now. Ask them what they think of it and whether they feel the same as you did when you were young.

Before you start this you might want to ask yourself some questions:

~ What sort of an example does your drug use set for your youngster today?

~ What are the good sides and bad sides of it?

~ Are there ways in which you could improve?

'You know that I tried LSD when I was young.'
                                                    – Parent

'I thought so. Look how you've turned out. I wouldn't touch the stuff myself.'   – 16 year old

3: BE CLEAR ABOUT YOUR OWN ATTITUDES TO DRUG USE

'We are all anti-drugs, aren't we? Now you tell me that we all use drugs, don't we? I get confused.' – Parent

Attitudes towards drug use are influenced by lots of things. These can include our experiences of drug use when we were young, stories in the media, our level of knowledge, our own insecurities. Most parents are against drug use when it involves young people and even more so when it involves their own youngsters. Some people go further and say that if we do not 'condemn' drug use then we must be 'condoning' it.

Unfortunately it is not that simple. Nearly everyone uses some sort of drug. We tend to accept our own drug use as normal but criticize other people for theirs.

Also, our attitudes tend to change over time. We may have different attitudes toward drug use than our parents, possibly different from the attitudes of parents of friends of our youngsters. Our attitudes to drug use are also likely to be different to those of our own youngsters. Drug use is a very complex issue.

So what are you supposed to think? A good place to start is to recognize where you stand and why. And be prepared for other people to have different views.

'Why should our attitudes to drugs be the same as our parents? Their experience was totally different. The drugs around today just weren't available to them.'

– 16 year old

Try this exercise. It might help you to think more about your own attitudes.

ACCEPTABLE OR UNACCEPTABLE?

Look at each of the situations below. Give each one a score out of a maximum of 10: 10 is totally acceptable; 0 is totally unacceptable. Keep a record of your score.

```
0    1    2    3    4    5    6    7    8    9    10
•••••••••••••••••••••••••••••••••••••••••••••••••••••
```
Totally unacceptable   Totally acceptable

←———   ———→

1. A 7 year old has a small glass of wine with their family over Sunday lunch.

2. A 17 year old smokes cannabis at their friend's house.

3. A 14 year old inhales an aerosol in the park with some friends.

4. A 15 year old comes home a bit drunk after going to a Christmas disco.

5. A 16 year old picks some magic mushrooms with some friends and eats them.

6. A 17 year old takes half a tablet of ecstasy in a nightclub and dances with friends till the early hours.

7. A 15 year old smokes 10 cigarettes a day.

8. A 17 year old injects heroin on a regular basis with their mate.

9. A 15 year old is prescribed tranquillizers by their doctor because they have become very anxious.

10. A 16 year old drinks at least 10 cups of coffee a day.

How many did you score on each question? Why did you score differently on different questions?

Discuss the attitude quiz with your partner, a friend or another parent and see what they think of your answers. Even better, try it with your youngster and see whether they share your ideas. Remember it is likely that there will be different views.

Now have a look through the following list of factors. How might these influence your attitudes to drug use?

~ your own experiences of drug use

~ the drug concerned (i.e. drug X is OK but drug Y is not)

~ whether it is legal or illegal to use the drug

~ the age of the young person

~ whether the user is male or female

~ who the user is with

~ what the drug user is doing at the same time as they are using (e.g. dancing or driving a car)

~ where you get your information from

How do each of these things influence your attitudes to drug use? What other things influence your attitudes to drug use?

What factors might influence your youngster's attitude? The next section may help you to talk about it with them.

●●●●●●●●●●●●●●●●●●●●●●●●●●●●●●●●●●●●●

4: TALK AND LISTEN TO YOUR YOUNGSTER

'My daughter wouldn't talk to me about it. But when I stopped and thought about it, I didn't really give her much chance.'
                                                              – Parent

Communication between parents and their youngsters sometimes breaks down when the youngsters are in their teens. There is often very little discussion and what discussion there is can end up as a shouting match. When it comes to drugs in particular, a lot of parents are very anxious talking to their youngster.

Many young people also find drug use a difficult subject to talk about with their parents. What if the parents find out that they are using drugs? What if they cannot agree? It is not surprising that a lot of parents and youngsters decide to avoid talking about drug use at all.

When parents do get round to talking about drug use

with their youngsters the danger is that they will do all the talking themselves. Quite often it will end up with something like, 'You wouldn't get involved in drugs would you?'

As well as talking to your youngster you need to *listen* carefully to what they have to say. Try to do it in such a way that they feel they can tell you what they are really thinking and feeling (this section will give you some help on how to achieve this). Be aware that they might also know a lot more about drugs than you do and be able to teach you more about it. You can learn a lot from them.

> *'My parents were happy to talk about drugs. The problem was they never stopped talking. They weren't so keen on listening to me. Every time I said something they didn't like they just hit the roof.'*
>
> – 16 year old

Try to leave them with the clear understanding that they can talk to you about drugs both now and in the future. The key is to not make discussion of drugs a big deal but an everyday matter where different views can be tolerated and exchanged.

> *'My advice is don't wait till a crisis to talk about drugs. Also don't make a big thing about it. Make it so it's a normal thing to talk about.'*   – Parent

> *'If you make a big deal about it they just clam up and it goes underground. I'd rather know what they do even if it means I sometimes have to bite my tongue.'*
>
> – Parent

Blocks to talking and listening

Some things which get in the way of effective talking and listening are:

Ordering – 'You must!' 'You have to!' 'You will!' 'You won't!'

Always advising – 'What you should do is … '

Put downs – 'You look stupid.' 'Other people will think you … '

Threats – 'If you don't stop I will … ' 'Wait till your father comes home!'

Lecturing – 'Sit there and listen to me!'

Diagnosing – 'What's wrong with you is … '

Undermining – 'You are nothing but a no good … !' 'You're just stupid!'

Moralizing – 'If you had any decency at all you would … '

Interrogating – 'Why?' 'Who?' 'When?' 'How?' 'Come on, tell me, admit it!'

Questions that have no good answer – 'You wouldn't, would you?' 'I suppose you think drugs are OK, don't you?'

Predicting – 'If you do that … will happen.' 'You *will* look silly!' 'If you carry on like this, you will … '

Patronizing – 'There, there. I'm sure it will be alright.'

Can you hear yourself speaking? Which ones do you use? What other things do you say or do to block effective communication? How could you improve?

Communicating effectively

Communicating effectively about drug use with your youngsters means:

1. Being honest about how you feel and why.
2. Not going over the top, shouting or over-reacting.
3. Not being too hypocritical. (Consider your own drug use both now and when you were young.)
4. Being flexible, agreeing to differ and being able to compromise.
5. Listening carefully to what they have to say.
6. Taking their ideas and feelings seriously.
7. Helping them reach their own decisions rather than always telling them what to do and think.
8. Being realistic about their drug use and behaviour. Fashions do change, as do views on what is or is not acceptable.
9. Not putting them down or always criticizing them.
10. Not making out you know things if you really don't know much.

It is difficult and we all have room for improvement.

Try this exercise with your youngster.

TALKING AND LISTENING – HOW GOOD ARE YOU?

1. Look through the list above together.
2. Go through each statement and for each item score yourself somewhere between 0 and 10, 0 being 'I'm hopeless at it' and 10 'I'm brilliant at it.'

3. Ask your youngster what score they would give you on each item.

4. Discuss how your scores compare with the score your youngster gives you. Also discuss how you could improve on each one.

5. Watch how you talk to each other over the next few weeks and see if you can both make some improvements.

But – don't expect too much of yourself. Remember, we are only human. Being a parent is difficult and often lonely. We all have room for improvement and of course the perfect parent does not exist.

● ●

5: PUT YOURSELF IN THEIR SHOES. WHAT IS IT LIKE TO HAVE YOU AS A PARENT?

'It's tough being a parent. There is no proper training for it even though it's probably one of the most difficult jobs going. There is no such thing as the "perfect parent" despite what they show in the glossy magazines. In the real world you just have to do your best.'
                – Parent

Being a teenager, youngster, adolescent – even the words feel a bit awkward – is difficult. Being a parent can also be difficult. Being the parent of an adolescent is even harder. In today's ever-changing, high pressure world, it is probably more difficult to be a parent than it has ever been before.

'They can't really win, can they? We expect them to be grown up but there is so much pressure on them these days – from us, their teachers, their mates. They

*probably feel everyone is watching them and passing
judgement on them all the time and I suppose they are
right.'*   – Parent

Adolescence is an in-between world. It is like sitting on a
fence but not being allowed in the attractive-looking gar-
dens on either side. You are not a child any more and not
expected or allowed to act like one. You have to be grown
up and sensible but you are not allowed to be too grown up
and sensible. You are not given the same rights, freedom,
independence and responsibilities as adults. Adolescence is
about transition and change – physical, emotional, eco-
nomic and social. But it is also about being in 'no man's
land'. It is about experimentation and discovery, finding
out what sort of person you are and what sort of person
you want to be.

This can be very exciting but also very scary and full of
contradictions. There are contradictions between the need
for independence and feelings of insecurity; between want-
ing to make your own decisions and yet feeling controlled
by others; between doing your own thing and yet being
constantly criticized.

*'What is it like being my age? Horrid. Now will you
close my door on your way out?'*   – 13 year old

Some of the things adolescents need are:

a chance to experiment	to be trusted
to be accepted for themselves	to do adult things
security	space of their own
for people to take an interest	to have friends
praise	to make their own
understanding	decisions

independence
to feel useful
appropriate affection
reasonable rules
  and limits
to test boundaries
flexibility
responsibility
their own privacy
to be successful
to be taken seriously
consistency
to be listened to

to choose their own
  friends
for it to be OK to fail
to be fashionable on
  their own terms
not to be embarrassed
to fit in with a crowd
not to be made to feel
  awkward
not to be always criticized
help and advice when
  asked for
to try out new things

THINKING ABOUT ADOLESCENCE

Have a look at the list of adolescent needs and consider the following points:

1. Would you add anything else? If so, what?
2. Which were important to you when you were an adolescent?
3. Which ones do you think are most important to your youngster?
4. How do you help them with these things?
5. How do you hinder them with these things or make matters worse?
6. What could you do to help them more and hinder them less?
7. What do the things on the list have to do with drug use by young people?

Try talking through the questions with your partner, a friend or another parent.

*'We all have room for improvement. When you stop
and look at yourself as a parent – if you can find the
time – you realize that you can go a bit stale. But you
can come up with new things to make it better. Not just
for them, but for yourself as well.'*   – Parent

*'When you think about what being young and growing
up involves I sometimes think it's a miracle that they
are not all out of their heads on drugs all the time.'*
          – Parent

WHEN I WAS YOUNG ...

*'Yes, I was young once but it all seems such a long
time ago. It seems like another person. You really
have to stop and think hard to remember. I suppose
my youngster is a bit of an angel compared to what I
used to get up to.'*   – Parent

What were you like as an adolescent? What did you find difficult?
What did you find most difficult about your parents? In what ways is
it different for today's youngsters?

Why not tell your youngster what it was like for you and see
what they think? Have the discussion with one of your own parents
in the room if you can, three generations all talking about these
issues together. What do you all think has changed for young people and what remains the same?

WHAT ABOUT YOUR NEEDS AS A PARENT?

You also have needs. You have a right to expect certain things from
your youngsters. Some of the things we want of them are very similar to the things that they need from us.

Have a look at the list of adolescent needs on pages 75–6. Which
of the things on the list do you want from them? What else do you
want from them? Some other possibilities are:

~ to know that they are OK

~ to know what they get up to

~ to know they think we are OK as parents

~ to have them understand it's not easy being a parent

~ to have them respect our views and values

Do you get the things you want from your youngster? If not, why not? Is it realistic to expect these things? If so, what could you do to make the situation better?

In order to gain a better understanding of these issues, try the next exercise with your youngster.

LIKES/DIFFICULTIES

1. **Parent**: Write down two lists on a piece of paper. The lists should be of **things you like** about your youngster and **things you find difficult** about your youngster. Make sure that the first list has more things on it than the second one.

2. **Youngster**: Write down two lists on a piece of paper. The lists should be of **things you like** about your parent and **things you find difficult** about your parent. Make sure that the first list has more things on it than the second one.

3. The next step is to tell each other what you have put on your lists. **Youngster**, go first. Explain the things you find difficult about your parent. **Parent**, listen carefully to your youngster. Do not interrupt them all the time. Don't get into discussing each thing on the list.

4. Now, **parent**, it's your turn. Tell your youngster about the things you find difficult about them. **Youngster**, you now have to listen without interrupting all the time. Again, don't get into a discussion.

5. **Youngster**, now you tell your parent about the things you like about them.

6. **Parent**, now you tell your youngster about the things you like about them.

7. It's a good idea to have a quiet period now, just to think about what has been said.

8. Now discuss what has been said. In particular:

   a) How do you both feel about what has been said?

   b) What can you **both** do to improve your relationship?

   c) How this could help when it comes to drugs?

9. Try to work out some definite things you can both do to make improvements. Why not make a date for a few weeks' time to check to see what has happened?

You might also like to look at some of the other sections in this book together. The next section is about making sure your youngsters have a good drugs education.

• •

6: MAKE SURE THEY HAVE A GOOD DRUGS EDUCATION

'I used to think it was best just to tell them to say no to drugs. I've learnt it's not that simple. My youngsters went through a stage when they did anything that I told them not to. To me it's not just whether they use a drug or not – it's how they do it, whether they know what they're doing and what happens to them.'

– Parent

'My idea that they would never use any illegal drug was a bit stupid really. When you think about how widespread drug use is, especially cannabis use, there's more than a 50/50 chance in my area that your kid will be involved at some time or other. You can either face it sensibly or force it underground.'

– Parent

A lot of people think that if we educate young people about drugs they will not use them. The problem is that drugs education does not stop young people using drugs. Research into the effects of drugs education on young people has found that:

1. Trying to shock or scare them off drugs does not work.

2. Telling them not to do it can even encourage some young people to use drugs. This is especially the case if authority figures like police officers, teachers or parents say don't do it.

3. Making a big thing of drug use is a mistake. It needs to be part of everyday discussion with young people.

4. Drugs education should not be delivered as a 'one off'. It needs to be part of a full programme of personal and social education.

5. Too often drugs information is distorted to make drug use seem worse than it is. Young people then find out from their own experience that it is not so bad. After this they will be very reluctant to trust adults again.

6. Trying to reduce the harm from drug use may be more achievable than trying to stop all use of drugs. It's a question of having realistic objectives.

7. There are no simple answers.

'Too many adults think that if young people are told not to use drugs or how awful it can be, then they won't use them. The problem is that most young people find out that it is not all bad. In fact many discover just the opposite – that drug use can be fun and brighten up their lives … and it's an even bigger buzz if your parents and teachers tell you not to.' — Teacher

A good drugs education should give young people:

~ Accurate factual information about the different drugs, their effects and risks. There should also be information on the workings of the law, the help that is available for drug users, etc.

~ A chance to work out their own attitudes to drug use and hear other people's views.

~ An opportunity to develop the ability to make their own informed choices about drugs.

~ A chance to voice their own opinions, listen to others, argue and debate.

~ The knowledge and skills to understand and help other people.

~ The ability to understand how complex the drugs issue is and the role of drugs in society.

Drugs education will not stop youngsters using drugs. However, it can make them better informed, more careful about what they do and encourage communication and openness about drug use.

As a parent you can play an important role in making sure your youngster has a good drugs education.

LEARN MORE TOGETHER

1. Ask your youngster about the different places they get their drugs information.

2. Ask them about the drugs education they have had at school or college. What has it consisted of, what do they think of it and how does it match up to what we said about drugs education at the beginning of this section?

3. Ask them what they would like to find out more about. Add in your own thoughts and questions. What do you want to know more about?

4. Discuss how you could work together to find out more.
   (Some sources of further information are listed in Appendix II
   of this book.)

5. What about working through some of the sections in this
   book together?

Support sensible drugs education at your youngster's school or college

Many teachers are very nervous about drugs education.
They think parents will disapprove unless it consists of
simple and hard-hitting anti-drugs messages. They probably know that this won't be effective, but they are sometimes not sure what other approaches they might use. Let
them know that they have your support for accurate and
sensible drug education which is designed to reduce the
harms from drug use.

A lot of schools have recently come across drug use by
students. Some have panicked because they think parents
will view their school as having a drugs problem. Hundreds
of youngsters have been expelled from school over drugs
incidents when there might have been better ways of handling the issue.

So here is an action plan for you. You could:

1. Ask about what is going on at your youngster's
   school. Give your support to realistic and sensible
   approaches towards drugs education.

2. Ask about how you might be able to help. This could
   include recommending that the school has a look at
   some of the resources we have listed in Appendix II.
   It might also include fundraising for new
   educational resources. Many schools have very little
   money to buy new training packs, videos, etc.

3. Raise the issue through the school's Parent Teachers Association. Many schools have organized drugs awareness workshops for parents. Some have been led by drug experts and teachers but some have also had parents and students taking a leading role. Some PTAs have also raised money to buy the much needed drugs education teaching resources.

4. Raise the issue with the school governors. Do they have a policy on personal, social and health education (PSHE) that includes drugs? What does it say? Is it any good? Is it being put into practice? Does the school respond sensitively to actual incidents of drug use by pupils?

What about elsewhere in the community?

Support other drugs education work for young people in your local community. This could include youth clubs and other youth and community organizations.

'It's silly really. We get more and more "Don't do drugs" and "Drugs kill" campaigns and at the same time more and more youngsters are using drugs. It's not the young people who need to think again. I think it's us. Clearly we have got it all wrong and need to be more honest and realistic.'   – Youth worker

7: AGREE SOME DRUG RULES WITH THEM

'Agree, compromise ... sometimes I don't think parents know what that means.'   – 18 year old

Your youngster needs to know what you expect of them when it comes to drugs. It is no good not telling them what you expect and then going mad when they do something you do not approve of. You need to establish some drug rules. But you will not make much progress by just announcing them. You need to discuss the proposed rules with your youngster. Try to reach some sort of agreement. You need to *negotiate* with them.

This means:

- ~ listening to what they have to say
- ~ being realistic
- ~ being prepared to compromise
- ~ agreeing to differ on some things

If the spotlight is going to be on their drug use it also makes sense to establish some rules about your own drug use at the same time. Your youngster is much more likely to follow the rules if they have had a hand in making them and the rules also apply to you.

Try this exercise.

NEGOTIATING DRUG RULES

1. Think about your youngster and the drugs they might be using now or be likely to come across in the next few months. Which drugs are they? Cigarettes, tea/coffee, alcohol, glue, gas/aerosols, cannabis, amphetamine, LSD, ecstasy, poppers?

2. For each of the drugs you want to make rules about write down the following:

   a) What rules should apply to each drug? It could be not using the drug at all or, if it is to be tolerated, some idea of how much is allowed, when, where, with whom, how often, etc. Do be realistic about what young people do. There is no point in setting rules they cannot and will not keep to.

   b) What should be the consequences of breaking the rules? You could include things like being grounded, fines, forgoing pleasant activities or taking on unpleasant activities.

3. Now ask your youngster to do the same exercise for your drug use. What do they think the rules, and consequences of breaking the rules, should be for **your** drug use?

4. Arrange a negotiation meeting with your youngster. Have your ideas ready and ask them to have theirs ready.

5. First agree **how** you will run the meeting. Remember what we said about negotiation before. It is supposed to be a process of give and take, of compromise and careful listening. It should be fair. If they are not to come home rolling drunk at midnight, then neither should you!

6. Who is going to start, you or them? Take it in turns to explain the rules and consequences of breaking the rules you have arrived at. Don't get bogged down arguing over any one rule until you have **both** been through your ideas.

7. Now apply the negotiation rules and look for areas where you can agree. You may need to modify your ideas. You may need to trade rules.

8. Once you have reached some agreement, write down what has been decided about rules and consequences of breaking them. Both agree to try to keep to the rules.

9. Set a date and time to discuss the rules again soon. You will need to check how you are both doing and decide whether any rules need changing.

'I tried this exercise with my dad. It was great. I'm happy to hear what he thinks I should do, so long as I can tell him about his drinking and smoking.'

– 16 year old

8: ANTICIPATE HOW YOU WOULD REACT IF THEY WERE USING DRUGS

'When we found out all we did was shout and argue. I argued with him about it. I fell out with my wife. If I'm honest, I caused more problems than his drug use ever did.'
                                     – Parent

Part III of this book, 'Coping in a crisis', page 107, gives practical advice for handling suspected or actual drug use by your youngster. For now, try to think about how you might react. What if you were to find what looks like some drugs in your youngster's bedroom? What if they came in drunk or high? What if they were to tell you straight that they have used an illegal drug? What if they have been using drugs heavily for a time?

It can be very scary for parents to think about these types of situations. It is also difficult to predict how we would actually react. However, it can be useful to force ourselves to think about how we *might* react, how we *should* react and how we definitely *should not* react.

WHAT WOULD YOU DO IF ... ?

Think about the situations below. If it was your youngster ...

    a) How would you feel?

    b) What would you be thinking?

    c) What would you actually do?

1. Your friend tells you that your 11 year old has been seen smoking cigarettes on the bus on the way to school.
2. Your 14 year old arrives home late one night drunk and smelling of booze.

3. You find a wrapper with a white/yellowish powder under your youngster's bed while you are emptying the bin from their room.

4. Your 16 year old is brought home by the police after being caught smoking cannabis on a street corner.

5. Your 18 year old regularly goes to clubs in the city centre. They return the next morning and sleep it off most of the next day. Recently they have been very moody and lacking in energy. Last week the local paper had an article in it about 'Ecstasy and the rave scene'. The way they described regular users sounds just like your youngster.

6. You are all watching a television soap which has included a story about young people smoking cannabis and taking LSD. The parents in the soap are really angry with their youngsters about it. Your 15 year old suddenly says, 'I don't know what the fuss is all about. Almost everyone I know uses cannabis.'

Now ...

1. Talk about the situations and your answers with your partner or a friend. What do they think of your reactions?

2. Talk about the situations with your youngster. How do they think a parent should react? What would they expect you to do in such situations? What do they think of your reactions to these case studies?

3. Draw up a list of dos and don'ts for a parent responding to their youngster's rumoured or actual drug use. The don't list is quite easy, partly because it is always easy to say what we should not do.

Some important dos include:

~ Listen to their side of the story.

~ Make sure you do deal with issues which come up and not just hope they will go away.

~ Tell them how you feel.

~ Keep calm.

Make your own list by thinking of the situations you looked at
before. (For more information on the dos and don'ts of coping in a
crisis see Part III of this book, page 107.)

4. Without being too hard on yourself, think about:

   a) which of the dos you would find difficult

   b) which of the don'ts you would easily fall into

   c) how you could improve your reactions

*'It's funny. I dreaded finding out he was using because
you hear so many terrible stories. But it was a relief
having it out in the open. It meant we could get on and
deal with it. We still don't agree about it but I can see
her point of view.'*   – Parent

● ●
9: LEARN BASIC FIRST AID SKILLS

What would you do if you found your youngster drunk, high,
stoned or hallucinating? Would you know what to do? And
what would you do if they had lost consciousness or stopped
breathing? Do you know enough about basic first aid?

We are not trying to scare you, but we do suggest that
you learn something about first aid. It is very unlikely that
you will come across your youngster unconscious after taking drugs. However, it could happen and knowing what to
do in an emergency can save lives.

If someone is heavily drunk, high or hallucinating and conscious ...

~ Don't try to talk about what has happened in any
  detail (wait till they have sobered up).

~ Keep an eye on them and don't leave them alone.

- ~ Sit them down in a quiet room. The half-sitting position is a good one (see diagram below).

- ~ Open a window to let in fresh air.

- ~ Talk quietly and calmly. Don't shout at them.

- ~ Help calm them down if necessary. Reassure them.

- ~ Loosen their clothing at the neck, chest and waist.

- ~ If they are cold, cover them with a blanket but make sure they do not get too hot.

- ~ Try not give them anything to eat or drink. If they insist on a drink, give small sips of lukewarm water only.

- ~ Do not move them unless it is essential.

- ~ Do not try to induce vomiting.

- ~ If you are worried at all about their condition, keep them awake for a while before allowing them to sleep. Don't leave them to 'sleep it off' unattended. Each year some young people get very drunk or stoned, go to sleep and start vomiting. If unattended, this can be very dangerous, even fatal.

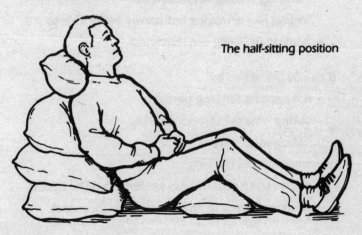

The half-sitting position

~ Call a doctor if you think it necessary. This requires some judgment by you. Try to err on the side of caution.

If someone is overheating/dehydrated ...

Drugs like ecstasy and amphetamine raise body temperature and give a boost of energy. If users take these drugs in hot places like clubs and dance for long periods they can loose a lot of body fluids. Overheating and dehydration can result. This can be very dangerous and has resulted in the death of a small number of young people in the UK.

The warning signs include:
~ feeling very hot and dehydrated
~ cramps in legs, arms and back
~ failure to sweat
~ headaches and dizziness
~ vomiting
~ suddenly feeling very tired
~ feeling like urinating but hardly being able to
~ fainting or losing consciousness

It can be prevented by:
~ not dancing for long periods
~ taking breaks between dancing
~ sitting in cool areas
~ wearing cool clothing
~ not wearing caps or hats as they keep the heat in
~ drinking plenty of fluids to replace those lost

~ avoiding alcohol and coffee (as they dehydrate even
  further)

If someone is overheating/dehydrating:

~ call an ambulance

~ move the person into a cool place (outside may be
  best)

~ splash them with cold water and fan them to cool
  them

If someone has lost consciousness ...

If someone has lost consciousness or you are having difficulty in waking them up, then call for professional assis-
tance. It is better to have an unnecessary doctor's visit
than a tragedy. If they are out cold, don't waste time with a
doctor. Call an ambulance out. In the meantime there are a
few ways in which you can help:

1. Clear the person's airway. Place one hand under
   their neck to support it. Put your other hand on
   their forehead and gently tilt their head backward.
   Push their chin upwards (see diagram overleaf).

2. Check to see whether they are breathing. Do this by
   checking if you can hear or feel their breaths. Put
   your ear against their nose and lips. Look to see if
   their chest or abdomen is moving.

IF THEY ARE BREATHING ...

1. Loosen their clothing at the neck, chest and waist.

2. Put them in the recovery position (see diagram on
   page 95).

3. Stay with them and keep checking their breathing. Get someone else to ring an ambulance.

4. If they come round, provide reassurance.

IF THEY ARE NOT BREATHING ...

Mouth-to-mouth resuscitation (the kiss of life) should be started straightaway (see diagram opposite).

1. Clear their mouth of any dirt or vomit.

2. Tilt their head back and lift their chin. Give them two slow, deep breaths.

3. Pinch their nose then take a deep breath in. Seal your lips around their mouth and blow into it. See that their chest rises as you blow in.

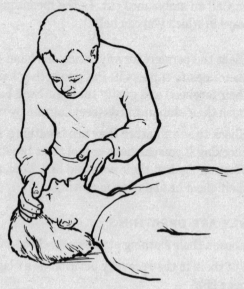

Clearing the airway

4. Take your mouth away and watch their chest fall.

5. Check their pulse to see whether their heart is beating. Do this by putting two fingers in the groove at the side of the Adam's apple and pressing firmly. If you can't feel a pulse within a few seconds their heart has stopped beating (see diagram on page 95).

IF THEIR HEART IS BEATING ...

1. Continue mouth-to-mouth. Do 16–18 breaths in each minute (about one every 3–4 seconds) until breathing starts again or the ambulance arrives.

2. When they start breathing again, put them into the recovery position (see page 95) and monitor their breathing.

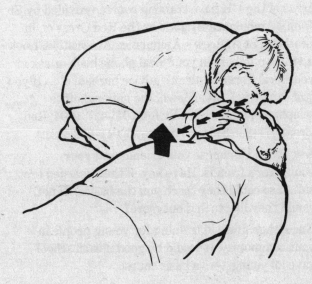

Mouth-to-mouth resuscitation

IF THEIR HEART IS NOT BEATING..

Heart resuscitation will be necessary.

This is more complicated and we recommend that you look it up in a specialist first aid manual or learn it through a proper first aid training course.

If you want to learn more about first aid ...

~ A good book is the *First Aid Manual* published by Dorling Kindersley. This is the authorized manual for St John's Ambulance Brigade and the Red Cross. It is available in many bookshops or at your local library.

~ Get some first aid training for yourself, your youngsters and other members of your family. Most areas of the UK have training course provided by St John's Ambulance Brigade or the Red Cross or, in Scotland, St Andrew's Ambulance Association. Look up their numbers in your local phone book or ask at your local library, citizen's advice bureau, etc. (If you still can't track them down, the national office telephone numbers are St John 071–251 0004; Red Cross 071–235 5454, St Andrew's 041–332 4031.)

~ Ask around amongst your friends and your youngster's friends. Have any of them learned first aid? If so could they teach you the basics? If not, would they like to find out more?

~ Encourage first aid training for young people in your community. It would be good if each school gave all youngsters a basic course.

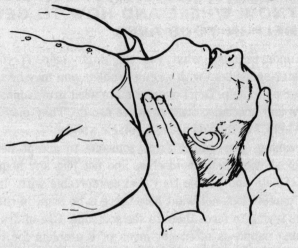

Checking the pulse

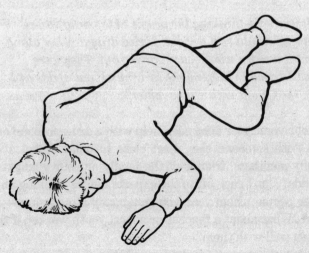

The recovery position

10: KNOW WHERE AND HOW TO GET HELP IN YOUR AREA

Don't underestimate what you can do to help. If your youngster needs help with a drug problem *you* may be the best person to help. Don't overestimate what professionals, experts and specialist drug agencies can do. They may be able to help, but they do not have magic wands.

Remember, you cannot force someone to accept help. They must want help themselves and not just any help – types of help and people they feel comfortable with. If a young person does not want help there is no point in their parents trying to force them to see someone. Use of drugs by young people is often not much of a problem for the young people themselves. Often it is the parent who needs the help for themselves – someone to talk through the issues with so that they understand their youngster and decide how best to respond.

> *'It was silly thinking the people at the drug advice project would sort her out. I tried dragging her along but it was me who needed sorting out. They were really good in helping me sort myself out and then I worked it out with my daughter.'* – Parent

If your youngster does need help with a drug problem or to talk with someone else, start close to home. What about family members, friends of the family or your youngster's friends? Don't rush off to the experts before thinking about other people whom your youngster may already know and trust. What about a teacher or a local youth worker, if they get on well with them?

What about your family doctor? How would your youngster feel talking to them? Talk to your youngster about who might be best to approach for help and whom they would feel most comfortable with.

> 'The thing is, you think if it's drugs, you need an expert. If it's really heavy perhaps you do, but often young people prefer to talk to people they already know and get on with. He talked it out with the youth club worker round the corner. The youth worker talked to me too. She was good and it helped.'   – Parent

On the other hand, your youngster might need or want the help of a drug expert. The important point is to involve them as much as possible in the decision. In fact, try to make it their decision.

Find out what help is available in your area

If not now, you or your youngster might need some expert help on drugs in the future. Why not find out now what sorts of help are available in your area? The different types of help include:

- ~ Drug advice and counselling services.
- ~ Services which offer prescribing of substitute drugs.
- ~ GPs/family doctors.
- ~ Hospital drug services which include treatment in hospital or on an out-patient basis.
- ~ Residential rehabilitation centres.
- ~ Needle exchange projects for drug injectors.
- ~ Self-help groups for drug users.
- ~ Self-help groups for parents.
- ~ Counselling services which specialize in working with young people around all issues, including drugs.

More information about these different types of service is included in 'What kind of help is available', page 52.

If you want to find out what help is available in your area for people who have drug problems or want expert advice or information you can:

~ Ask at your local citizen's advice bureau, doctor's surgery, library, council offices, social services, school or youth and community centre.

~ Ring SCODA (Standing Conference on Drug Abuse) on 071–928 9500. They keep records of specialist drug services in each area of the country.

~ Ring the Regional Health Information Service available on a national freephone number 0800–66 55 44. This should have details of local drug services as well as the full range of health services.

~ Ring Release, who run a 24-hour national helpline specially for people who have been arrested for a drug offence. They also give legal and social advice to parents. They can be contacted on 071–603 8654.

~ And don't forget to ask your youngster. They may know about local drug services. They may also be able to help you find out more.

What should you find out about services?

Once you find out the name and address or phone number of the drug services in your area, don't feel shy about finding out more. Some questions to ask them include:

~ What exactly do they offer?
~ How can they help young people?

~ How can they help parents?

~ When are their opening hours?

~ Can people refer themselves or do they have to go through a doctor or anyone else?

~ Is it drop in service or do you need an appointment? If an appointment is necessary is there a waiting list and how long is it?

~ Do they see people at an office base or do they do home visits?

~ Is there any age limit? Will they see under 16s?

~ Will they see youngsters without their parents being involved?

~ What do they do about confidentiality and records? (Most projects are very strict on confidentiality and do not tell anyone else.)

~ If your youngster goes, do they tell you what happened?

~ Are the staff used to working with youngsters?

~ Can you get any leaflets or other information about the project?

~ Can they suggest any other local services which might help young people and parents about drugs?

'Too many parents and young people seem to take whatever we offer. We are more experienced at working with older drug users who are often injectors. We need the younger ones and parents to tell us more about what they want and how we can help them. I wish they would tell us more. After all, we are here to help them.'
                                              – Drug project worker

WHEN YOUR YOUNGSTER NEEDS OR WANTS TO USE EXPERT DRUG SERVICES

~ Involve them as much as possible in the decisions.

~ Make sure they understand what is on offer.

~ Make sure they know how the service operates on things like confidentiality.

~ Try to get them to think about what they want and what might help them.

~ Encourage them to do the talking.

~ Talk about how you can best support them – should you go along, should you go along together, etc.?

~ If they are seen by themselves, don't nag them to tell you what happened.

~ If they are seen by themselves, don't expect the staff to tell you what they talked about with your youngster.

~ Don't expect miracles.

'I was too shy to ask for help even though things were really bad and we needed it. I kept thinking about what people would think of us – we like to think we're a good family. Well, I soon discovered that we are pretty average like most families. My advice to other parents is if you really need information, advice or help grab it and don't hang around.'   – Parent

11: BECOME ACTIVE IN YOUR LOCAL COMMUNITY

'We don't ask enough questions – the really difficult questions like what is being done about drug use, why, what effect will it have, both good and bad, is it a good use of money? After all, when you think of it – police, schools, health, councils, MPs – there's a lot of hot air and it's our money that they're spending.' – Parent

The drugs issue is very complex and affects everyone in some way or other. What may be fun and pleasurable for one group of people can be a great source of anxiety and cause problems for others. Some users are damaging themselves and cause problems in their communities. Some users want to stop or moderate their use and can be helped to do so within the community.

Some users are involved in theft and burglary to fund their use of drugs. Some drugs, especially alcohol, will be implicated in violent behaviour, including much male violence towards women and children. In some areas drug dealing has resulted in open gang warfare. In others, groups of youngsters using drugs on the street are seen as the main problem. In yet other areas, the drug problems mostly take place behind closed doors.

No wonder drugs is such an emotive and complex issue. This makes it so important to think carefully and try to develop realistic ways of cutting down on the problems. Too often in the past people have oversimplified the issue and tried to find solutions which have either been completely unsuccessful or themselves caused new problems.

For example, telling schools to get tough on drugs has resulted in more schools suspending or expelling youngsters for drug use. This confirms the youngster as an outcast, may create anti-heroes and will certainly not eliminate drug use, although it may force it underground.

Sending a heavy police presence into an area can disrupt supplies but will, almost certainly, move them into other areas. Even when the supply of one drug is restricted people often move on to other, sometimes more dangerous drugs.

In some areas there have even been local 'anti-drugs vigilante groups'. The effects of such groups are rarely as intended. They may merely push drug use underground or move it on to neighbouring areas, making it more difficult to deal with problems when they arise. They can also result in a vicious circle of escalating violence. Whilst such efforts are understandable, they are not generally helpful.

But this is not a counsel of gloom. Whilst there are no simple 'solutions' to the drugs problem there are lots of ways that you can usefully contribute to helping in your local community. We have already mentioned ways you might work with your schools, colleges and youth projects (see 'Make sure they have a good drugs education', page 79). Some other things you might do are:

1. Find out what local organizations are doing about the drugs issue. You could ask local specialist drug services, health service units, the local council, the police, MPs, etc. and tell them your views.

2. Talk to other parents and young people in your street and see what they think. Have they got enough information? Could you get some leaflets for them or arrange for a discussion or talk?

3. Find out about local services (see 'Know where and how to get help in your area', page 96) and campaign to help improve services for young people – especially education and help/counselling services.

4. Volunteer to help with local drug projects. It could be fundraising, decorating, counselling, etc.

5. Start up a parents' education or support group.

6. Talk to other people and help educate them.

7. Help develop good local leisure and education facilities for young people.

DRUG MYTHS QUIZ ANSWERS

From page 62.

1. **False**. We don't think a couple of drinks are dangerous. The same can be said about other drugs. It depends on what is taken, how much, the mood of the person and what they are doing at the time. (See 'What effects do drugs have and what are the real dangers?', page 26, for more on drug risks.)

2. **False**. Use of alcohol and tobacco can be very dangerous. These legal drugs claim tens of thousands of lives each year in the UK.

3. **True**. More than 20,000 people die each year from the effects of alcohol in the UK. The figure for heroin is under 200. There are about 100,000 premature deaths a year from the effects of tobacco. The figure for solvents (glue/gas, etc.) is about 150. There are almost no deaths directly attributable to cannabis use, although it can increase the risk of accidents, for example, motor accidents.

4. **False**. Over 2 million people in the UK have tried cannabis and the overwhelming majority have never been near heroin. There is no inevitable step from one drug to another.

5. **True**. Only a small percentage of people who use drugs – any drugs – come to serious harm. Most users enjoy their drug use. Some users try it and decide it is not for them. We hear most about the extreme cases. This is not to say that it is OK to use illegal drugs, but we do need to be honest

about their effects. Exaggerating the harm causes mistrust between adults and young people. We should try simply to tell the truth, the whole truth and nothing but the truth about difficult issues like drugs.

6. **False**. Users don't get hooked straightaway. Dependence, if it does develop, takes time. It can also vary a lot from person to person depending on their personality and situation. (See 'Why do young people use drugs?', page 10.)

7. **False**. Some of the heaviest users of drugs will commit crimes to finance their habits, but most drug users do not.

8. **False**. Not all youngsters try illegal drugs but the numbers of those who do is going up. In some areas there may even be a majority of 16 year olds who have tried an illegal drug or solvents at least once. In a survey in Liverpool and the Wirral in 1992 over 30 per cent of 15 to 20 year old males had tried cannabis, ecstasy or LSD.

9. **True**. Some leaflets list signs and symptoms of drug use but most of the symptoms listed are examples of normal behaviour, for example being moody or tired. Symptoms like these can be due to many reasons other than drug use. Unless a youngster is under the influence at the time you will probably see no clear signs of drug use. (See 'How can you tell if your youngster is using drugs?', page 45, for more on the signs and symptoms of drug use.)

10. **True**. The idea of the evil drug dealer is a bit of a myth. In most cases drugs are 'pulled' rather than 'pushed'. In other words, people go looking for them. Drug dealers do exist but most youngsters get drugs from friends and acquaintances. (See 'Where do young people get drugs from?', page 14.)

11. **False**. It's true that most cocaine, heroin and cannabis is imported from abroad but cannabis can be grown in the UK and drugs like amphetamine, LSD and ecstasy are often manufactured here.

12. **True**. Illegal drugs are not always that expensive when compared to alcohol. This is especially the case for drugs like cannabis and LSD.

13. **False**. Who are the 'wrong sort' of youngsters? We never think that we, or our youngsters, are the wrong sort. Illegal

drug use is now to be found in every sector of society, every social class, both sexes and every ethnic group. The search for a scapegoat to blame for the spread of drug use amongst young people is a waste of time.

14. **True** (probably). It is a safe bet that you use some drugs, perhaps caffeine (in tea, coffee, soft drinks and some chocolate), medical drugs, tobacco or alcohol. Yet we always tend to think other people use drugs rather than ourselves.

15. **False**. One problem is that most drug use is not that dangerous, so telling young people it is often gets them thinking we are lying to them or don't know what we are talking about. Their own experience and friends may tell them different things. Knowing the real facts is important so that people can make informed decisions and know exactly what they are doing. The research evidence shows that trying to shock or scare young people off drugs does not work and can sometimes be counterproductive.

How did you do? If you got less than eight right you might want to have a look back at Part I.

Part III

•••••••••••••••••••••••••••••••••••

Coping in a crisis

•••••••••••••••••••••••••••••••••••

WHAT CAN YOU DO?

'What can I do? I must do something, but what? How could they do that? What did I do wrong that they want to do drugs? Oh my God ... what if ... ?'

Faced with a youngster using drugs many parents react with fear, anger or guilt – sometimes all three. One after the other, the questions swirl around, building up the pressure. The real enemy in this situation is the urge to do something drastic – anything – that will make the problem go away. Frustration and a sense of powerlessness can turn into anger and guilt and may lead to over-reaction.

So what can you do? The first thing is to recognize that all these feelings are normal reactions in such stressful situations. Here is a list of some common reactions and feelings on learning of drug use:

~ panic
~ fearing the worst
~ exaggerating the dangers
~ getting very angry
~ going over the top
~ thinking something drastic has to be done straightaway
~ trying to ignore it or pretend it hasn't happened
~ arguing with partners or other family members over it
~ blaming it on yourself and feeling guilty
~ blaming it on other youngsters
~ blaming it on drug dealers
~ trying to keep it a secret

~ thinking there is no one else who's ever experienced
  it before
~ thinking there is no one who understands or can help
~ thinking a drug 'expert' can sort it all out

Try not to give in to the fear or anger. Instead, give yourself time to think. Try to keep calm. Create some space and
time for yourself. What is it that really demands an instant
response? If there is a youngster flat out on the floor, then
swift action is certainly needed (see 'Learn basic first aid
skills', page 88). But most other situations can wait a bit
whilst you get your own thoughts sorted out.

Get some support. You don't have to tackle these problems on your own. Is there another family member or close
friend with whom you can talk these things through? Be
careful to pick out the most level-headed person you know.
The last thing you need at this stage is being wound up by
someone even more scared of the situation than you are.

If you don't have a friend or relative who would be calm
enough to help you through this, there will probably be a
doctor, a teacher or maybe a youth worker who might be
able to help. There are a wide range of other people who
might also be able to help you through the crisis. Have a
look at 'Know where and how to get help in your area',
page 96, for advice on getting professional help.

Create some space for listening carefully to what your
youngster has to say. This is explored in more detail below
and in Part II of this book. The rest of this section tackles
the sort of crises which parents often worry most about.

> 'It was a real crisis, but we all worked at it and pulled
> together. In time it got better, in fact we all got on
> better than we had before.'   – Parent

What can you do if you suspect that your youngster may be using drugs?

'I thought something was up but I kept saying to myself I was imagining things. I left it for far too long before saying something and then when I did it came out all wrong. I was really worried about them but it just came out like a big attack on them. That is not how I should have handled it.'   – Parent

First principles are: keep calm – and check your facts. Who says that your youngster is taking drugs? Are you sure? Have a look at 'How can you tell if your youngster is using drugs', page 45. Remember it is important to communicate with your youngster, rather than just trying to spot the 'hidden signs and symptoms'. Likewise, if you have found a suspicious substance or object, look at 'What do different drugs look like?', page 41, and take care not to jump to the wrong conclusion.

You will also need to inform yourself about drugs and their use. If you rush straight off to tell your youngster about the horrors of drug use you could find yourself in the uncomfortable situation of realizing that they know more about it than you do. You might like to read through Part I and Appendix I of this book to get some information first.

You will then need to talk to your youngster. Part II contains lots of ideas on how to talk to young people so that they listen and how to listen so that they talk. If you suspect they are using drugs, do not jump in heavy-handedly and accuse them outright. Saying 'You're using drugs aren't you?' is not a good starting-point.

'When they found out they just thought the worst. They accused me of all sorts I hadn't done. I understand

*they don't like what I did, but they could have listened
to me.'* – 17 year old

Equally, don't go to the other extreme and try to pretend
you are not worried. Tell them about what you are concerned about and why. Show that you are concerned about
their welfare and that you care about them. Try to keep
calm about how you tell them and be prepared to listen to
what they have to say. Be prepared to be wrong in your
suspicions. Also realize that even if they are using they
may find it difficult to tell you straightaway.

*'My advice to parents if they suspect but aren't sure is
don't jump in with both feet. Think about it first. Talk
it through with someone else first. Think carefully
about exactly what you are going to say and carefully
choose when to do it. Don't let it get out of hand.
Overreacting just does not work.'* – Parent

What can you do if your youngster comes home stoned, high or drunk?

Keep calm is the first advice. If you do feel angry, try to
manage the way you react. Anger is a natural response,
but it can make things worse. Try to deal at a practical
level. Are they flat out or just woozy? If they are having
difficulty staying awake, don't let them 'sleep it off'. They
may be in danger of a potentially fatal overdose or choking
on their vomit – even on alcohol. If they are agitated or disorientated, try to calm them down. If they literally pass out
and you cannot rouse them, you must put them into the
recovery position (see page 95) and call an ambulance. It is
better to be safe than sorry. There are more practical hints
on dealing with an intoxicated youngster in the first aid
section, page 88.

Leave discussion about the rights and wrongs of the situation until the following day. You will be calmer and they will be sober. You will just be wasting your time trying to have a rational discussion with someone who is stoned or drunk.

The day after is the time to discuss rules for living together (see 'Agree some drug rules with them', page 84). You have the right not to have your home regularly disrupted by drunken or stoned behaviour. Fortunately, it is only a small minority of young people who will use frequently in this way.

> *'He came in completely out of his head. We tried to talk it out with him there and then. It just became a shouting match and he didn't know what he was saying. It's best to leave it till they are sober. The trouble is you feel annoyed with them there and then and it's hard being caring towards them. You have to look after them though to check out they are OK.'*
> – Parent

What can you do if your youngster is suspended or expelled from school for drug use?

> *'It can be really scary having the head teacher and school governors accusing your kid and almost accusing you of being a bad parent. She did take a bit of cannabis into school. That was wrong and I agree she should be punished for it. But the way they went about it was like a murder enquiry – way over the top. It didn't do any good for her, for the rest of the kids or for us as a family. She did wrong but she needed us to help her get through it and learn from it.'*   – Parent

Each year a few hundred youngsters in the UK – maybe more – are suspended or expelled from school for drug use. If this happens to your youngster the first step is to try and find out what really happened. Don't assume that your youngster is in the wrong. Mistakes are made, and a surprising number of suspensions and expulsions are based on hearsay and other evidence that would be inadmissible in a court of law.

Try to discuss the issues calmly with your youngster. They will probably be frightened of your response and it will not help if you are angry and shout at them. Have a look at the section 'Talk and listen to your youngster', page 70, for advice on talking and listening about drugs. Also, if they have not already spoken with you, discuss the matter with the relevant school staff. Ask them what they think happened and about the evidence they have to back it up.

A suspension is one thing and your youngster may be back at school quickly. An expulsion – or permanent exclusion – is obviously more serious. When you have a clear idea of what has happened you can decide if you want to accept an expulsion or whether to appeal. If you decide to appeal, the first step will be to make an appointment to see the head teacher or their deputy. It might be possible to persuade them to change their mind in favour of another punishment, even if your youngster has broken the rules.

Most suspensions or expulsions involve the possession or sale of illegal drugs, although a few have been because a youngster refuses to tell tales on another (drug using) schoolfriend.

Schools will rightly want to give out clear messages that illegal drug use is unacceptable, but to do this it is not necessary to expel every youngster who uses an illegal drug. If schools were to catch every youngster using illegal

drugs between the ages of 13 and 18 they might end up
expelling up to a third of all their pupils! There is no automatic rule requiring schools to expel youngsters in this
way. It is a matter of local policy and policy can be changed.

Even if an expulsion is confirmed by the school, you have
the right of appeal. In the state sector this appeal will
involve the Board of Governors of the school and the Local
Education Authority (LEA). The exact way the appeal will
work will vary from area to area. Sometimes the young
person involved and their parents will have to attend a
meeting of the school governors to try to convince them
not to go ahead with the expulsion. The LEA may have an
advisory teacher with a special interest in drugs issues
who might be able to help you and will also have officers
whose job it is deal with cases such as these.

You will have a difficult decision to make about a possible
appeal. Even if you win the appeal – and the odds may be
against you – do you want to subject your youngster and
your family to the controversy surrounding such a case?
The local media may pick the story up – 'School drug scan-
dal' might seem a very attractive story to them. Sometimes
it can seem easier to let the matter be dealt with quietly
and quickly get your youngster into another school.
However, if you do not want to do this or there are no suit-
able schools nearby, you should feel free to lodge an appeal.
When under 16s are expelled they still have a right to
full-time education. Your LEA should help with arrangements for entry to another school, but no school has an
automatic duty to accept any youngster. You may have to
shop around. For over 16s there is no automatic right to
education.

You might be able to get specialist advice on how to cope
with this situation from your local drug agency but not all
drug agencies are experienced in dealing with such cases.

See 'Know where and how to get help in your area', page 96, for more information.

> *'It is important in these situations that parents support their youngsters. Schools have a tendency to go over the top about drugs. I have been involved in a number of situations which have been like kangaroo courts and the head teachers have not known what they are talking about. One kept confusing cannabis and cocaine and kept mixing up which youngsters were involved.'* – Drugs education worker

What can you do if your youngster is arrested for a drug offence?

Youngsters under the age of 17 are only supposed to be interviewed by the police in the presence of a parent or guardian. Over 17s are treated as adults and parental involvement is not necessary. Your first involvement might be the police coming to the door or telephoning to ask you to come to the police station. Parents in this situation are often torn between their loyalty to their youngster and their desire to co-operate with and support the police.

The first step is to keep calm and to try to find out what has actually happened. Ask your youngster for their version of what has happened rather than assuming the police have got everything 100 per cent correct. Ask to talk to them without a police officer being present.

The police may let your youngster go without charging them. They may issue a caution. This often happens these days for first offences involving small quantities of illegal drugs for personal use, especially with cannabis.

If the police arrest your youngster, the young person has a right to a solicitor. It is a very good idea to get a solicitor.

You are not acting badly if you insist on having one present during any discussions with the police. You will probably be under great stress in such a situation and an experienced solicitor will know how to advise you best. If you don't have one already, the police will have a list of duty solicitors whose job it is to turn out in just such cases.

If the arrest is the first indication of any involvement with drugs by your youngster, you will probably be quite shell-shocked and need some time to work out how to handle the situation. Try to give yourself that time. Don't be pressured into hasty decisions which both you and your youngster might regret later. Your first decision might not be the best one. Asking for some time to discuss it in private and using a solicitor helps to keep your options open.

At the police station your youngster will have been seen by the custody officer whose job it is to complete and keep up-to-date the custody record. This is an important document which will have on it the details of the arrest, the reasons for the arrest and why the person arrested has been detained. The starting time of detention is also recorded there. Sometimes the police will ask you to sign this record to say that you do not want a solicitor. The legal rights organization Release advises those arrested never to sign away their rights to a solicitor.

An arrest will be a very stressful experience for both your youngster and for yourself. Try to support them and do what is best for them. Don't start having a go at them about what they have done. There will be plenty of time to discuss what has happened later. The most important thing straightaway is to deal with the legal situation.

'It can be very scary and intimidating having to go down to the police station. We all know it's best to keep calm but it is difficult exercising your rights even

*when you know what they are. I suppose I felt it was
me who had been caught rather than my son. I felt
angry with him and guilty myself so I felt I couldn't
ask for things or really stick up for him. Thinking
about it, we should have asked them more questions
and taken more time about answering their questions.
And solicitors? My advice is, if it is getting serious,
get a solicitor quick.'* — Parent

What can you do if your youngster is using drugs and doesn't see any harm in it?

This can be very difficult to cope with. Despite your best
efforts your youngster starts to use drugs. They enjoy it
and if you tell them not to they ignore you. They think you
know next to nothing about drugs and they may be right.
It is hard work being a parent. It can be really stressful
just having a young person growing up beside you in
your home. They see the world through their eyes not
yours, whatever you do or say. Sometimes even when
they are completely wrong they have to learn for themselves and make their own mistakes. There is no way
they are going to do something – or not do something –
just on your say so.

It can be terribly frustrating to have to sit on the side-
lines whilst someone you love does something stupid or
puts themselves at risk – deliberately, it seems. Yet, if we
are honest, weren't we just like that when we were
younger? Even if we weren't, it doesn't alter the fact that
young people can be headstrong. They are in such a hurry
to consume the world and all its pleasures that they have no
time to take care of themselves the way we want them to.

So what can you do? Well, first find out more. Have a
look through the first part of this book for general refer-

ence, pages 2–58, and look up the drugs they are using in Appendix I, 'Facts about drugs', page 127. This will tell you more about the risks they might be running. Then have a look at your own attitudes and maybe your own use of drugs ('Think about your own use of drugs', page 63, and 'Be clear about your own attitudes to drug use', page 68). Try to understand their situation – 'Put yourself in their shoes. What is it like to have you as a parent?', page 74, might help.

Then take your courage in your hands and ask them to describe to you just what it is they are getting out of their drug use. Use 'Talk and listen to your youngster', page 70, for ideas on how to talk and listen to your youngster about drugs and 'Agree some drug rules with them', page 84, for an exercise on setting rules about drugs. Make it clear to them that you want to try to understand it from their point of view.

You will need to set clear rules if the drugs are being used in your home. For example, you could be liable under the Misuse of Drugs Act if you permit or tolerate the smoking of cannabis in your home. 'What does the law say?', page 35, will give you background information on the legal situation and the rule setting exercise on pages 84–5 can help to agree drug rules with your youngster about use in the home.

Depending on the drugs your youngster is using and their methods of use you might want to check out if they are using in the least harmful way possible. This *harm reduction* approach is the one most often used by drug agency workers. They will work with a client to identify the most serious risks and make sure that the client knows how to avoid them.

With cannabis, for example, the risks include unsafe sex whilst stoned and being caught by the police and getting a criminal record. With heroin, injecting is the biggest risk, for sharing injecting equipment exposes the injector to blood-borne diseases like hepatitis and the HIV virus. Appendix I provides harm reduction advice for situations in which people continue to use drugs.

It should also be stressed again here that in most cases the use of illegal drugs will be recreational. By far the largest numbers of drug users today are those using drugs like cannabis, LSD and ecstasy on nights out, at parties, in clubs and so on. Most of these users will take good care of themselves and come to no lasting harm. This is not the same as accepting their behaviour, but it is true.

Finally, don't close the door on further discussion with your youngster even if you cannot see eye to eye with them. Leave them with the understanding that you will always be ready to talk to them again. One of the big problems with drug use is that it can undermine communication between young people and their parents. Points of view are often different, but that doesn't mean that we cannot keep talking.

> 'You can't live their lives for them even if you'd like to. I don't like her using but at least I know she is and I know something about it now. We do talk about it and I understand why she does it. I'm not happy about it. I never will be, but at least I know she knows what she's doing.'
> – Parent

What can you do if your youngster is using drugs heavily?

Heavy drug use probably involves at least daily use of either sedative drugs like heroin or stimulants like amphetamine. Using at such levels may involve injecting the drugs, although there a good number of daily users of heroin and amphetamine who do not inject. Heavy use can also involve solvents and sometimes other drugs.

It should be stressed that most drug users do not use in a heavy dependent way. It is only a minority who become so-called 'addicts'. For a full discussion of different levels of drug use see 'Why do young people use drugs?', page 10, but it is important to say here that the motives for heavy dependent drug use will be different from those for other types of more controlled drug use.

Faced with heavy drug use by their youngsters, parents have tried many different ways of coping. Some have tried to supervise their youngster closely in an attempt to stop them obtaining drugs completely or to moderate their use. This has involved locking them in rooms, trying to keep them in the house or spying on them wherever they go.

Other parents have tried to cut off drug supplies by involving the police or directly confronting dealers. Some have even gone out to buy drugs for their youngster in an attempt to limit their use.

Some parents have arranged for their youngster to move elsewhere in the hope that a new place and new friends and situation will break the pattern of drug use.

Although some of these measures are not ones we would recommend, it would be wrong of us to condemn these parents. They were trying their best in very difficult circumstances. Sadly, there is no one right way of responding to heavy dependent drug use. Some strategies work in some situations with some drug users and others don't.

Dependent drug users often have underlying social or emotional problems from which the drug use may represent an attempted escape. Heavy drug use can also produce its own problems of physical and psychological dependency, legal difficulties and chaotic lifestyle. These become overlaid on the existing problems of the user and the resulting complex of problems can be very difficult to unravel.

If your youngster has such a complex pattern of drug use, underlying problems and chaotic lifestyle, you would be well advised to seek specialist help. Your family doctor may be able to help if you think they will be sympathetic. Also help can be arranged from community based drug advice services. Details of these services and how to use them are in 'What kind of help is available?', page 52, and 'Know where and how to get help in your area', page 96. You can also get details of local services from your regional health information service by ringing the 0800 66 55 44 number.

The drug advice agency or family doctor will be able to work with your youngster if they are willing to accept their help. Unfortunately, if the user does not want help there is little that can be done for them. If the young person concerned is under 16 years of age the drug agency may be reluctant to get involved and advise you to contact the social services department instead. They may be worried that exposing your young person to the older and more experienced addicts on their caseload may make things worse. In any event drug agencies should be able to advise you and help you cope better with the situation.

'It is especially difficult for parents when their youngsters get into really heavy use. They tend to blame themselves, which does not help anyone. Sometimes they try to cover it up and end up colluding with their child. They often forget themselves and the help they need for themselves. There are no simple solutions and what is best in one situation may not be best in another.'
— Drug agency worker

What can you do if your youngster is violent on drugs or steals your money or possessions to buy drugs?

Both of these are thankfully rare although they do happen. Parents in this situation need help for themselves and their youngster. Understandably they struggle to cope with such awful behaviour. It seems the ultimate betrayal and the parents are caught between their love for their youngster and their horror and anger at how they are being treated.

We believe that it does not help to start making excuses for the young person in this situation. Violence, abusive behaviour and stealing from the family home are unaccept-able. We all have the right not to be abused in such a way. Just because someone is using or even dependent on drugs does not excuse such behaviour. Whilst there are those who would say that heavy drug users or 'addicts' are not responsible for their actions, we do not take such a view.

It is important to understand the terrible dilemmas of parents caught up in this situation. But too much kindness in the face of abuse can sometimes make things worse. Long-suffering parents putting up with awful behaviour from their youngsters are a poor role-model for them. When the youngster hits the outside world and treats others in the way they have learned to treat their parents, they can end up in terrible trouble or even in prison. So by trying to be too kind and accepting behaviour that is really unacceptable, parents can be setting up their youngster for trouble later on.

In the short term, the key task is to create some space and time to take stock of what has happened. You may need someone to talk to and support you, just as your youngster also needs help. With a young person under 17 the social services department may be able to give you advice. There are also specialist drug agency workers who may have worked with parents before in similar situations. See 'Know where and how to get help in your area', page 96, and Appendix II, the resources section, for information on getting help.

If you are able to arrange some help for your youngster, be aware that this will only work out if they see themselves as having a real problem and want help themselves. At some stage it might even be necessary to exclude the young person from the family home. Most parents would resist doing this to the bitter end, but sometimes it is the only immediate answer. Some parents have called in the police in such situations or with under 17s arranged with social services to have them taken into care.

'It was terrible. It needed drastic action and I needed some help as much as they did. I felt awful about myself and blamed myself. I felt it was all my fault and then I felt terribly guilty about getting them to leave. But it couldn't have gone on any longer. Looking back, it was the right thing to do.'   – Parent

Part IV

●●●●●●●●●●●●●●●●●●●●●●●●●●●●●●●●●●●●

Conclusion

●●●●●●●●●●●●●●●●●●●●●●●●●●●●●●●●●●●●

To conclude the book we wish to emphasize a number of key points. These are:

1. Keep drugs in perspective – don't exaggerate, overreact or panic.

2. Be aware of your own values and beliefs about drugs. Think carefully about where you stand and why and appreciate that other people, including your youngster, may have different views.

3. Increase your knowledge and awareness of drugs, but don't underestimate what you already know.

4. Distinguish between fact and myth. You don't have to become a drugs expert, but don't fall for the many myths which commonly surround discussion of drug use.

5. Try to appreciate what life is like for your youngster and what drug use – legal or illegal – may mean to them.

6. Talk to your youngster about drugs and listen carefully to what they have to say. Don't make discussion of drugs a big thing, but make sure they know that you are prepared to listen to them now and in future.

7. Feel free to seek out specialist help and advice if you and/or your youngster need it.

8. Don't become isolated. Talk to other people, especially other parents, about the drugs issue.

As we said in the introduction, we value your views about this book. If you have any comment you wish to relay to us or have other ideas about educating parents about drugs, write to us at the address given on page xiii.

Appendix I

●●●

Facts about drugs

●●●

INTRODUCTION

'I talk to a lot of parents about drugs. They nearly always underestimate what they know.'

– Drug project worker

Lots of parents think that they know nothing about drugs but discover that they actually know quite a lot. To help further, this part of the book is for reference. It contains information about the following drugs:

alcohol

amphetamines

barbiturates

caffeine

cannabis

cocaine and crack

ecstasy

heroin (and other opiates)

LSD

magic mushrooms

nitrites (poppers, liquid gold)

solvents (glues, gases, aerosols, etc.)

tobacco

tranquillizers

other drugs (ketamine, PCP and OTC medicines)

For each drug we give information about what it is, what its street names are, how it might be used medically, how it is taken, the extent of its use and its effects and risks.

There is also advice about reducing harm for people who will continue to use drugs whatever is said. The best way to reduce the harm from drugs is, of course, not to use at all, but some people will always choose to carry on using drugs and we have to be realistic about this. The reducing harm advice will keep users as safe as possible until they decide to stop.

If you need to know about the legal status of drugs, refer to 'What does the law say?', page 35. If you need even more information about the drugs themselves, refer to the books or organizations listed in Appendix II, 'Where to find out more', page 165.

● ●
ALCOHOL

WHAT IS IT?
Alcohol is a liquid containing ethyl alcohol. It is made by the fermentation of fruits, vegetables or grains.

STREET NAMES
Booze, drink, bevvy; individual types: beer, lager, wine, spirits, etc.

MEDICAL USE
None. In the past alcohol was given to hospital patients to help with a good night's sleep.

HOW TAKEN
Alcohol is swallowed as a drink.

EXTENT OF USE
Over 90 per cent of British adults drink alcohol at least on an occasional basis. There are many young regular users.

More than 60 per cent of young people will buy alcohol illegally. There are over 170,000 licensed outlets for the sale of alcohol in the UK.

EFFECTS

Alcohol is a sedative drug. It slows down body functioning. Small amounts make users more relaxed and less inhibited. More can lead to poor co-ordination and slurred speech, double vision and ultimately loss of consciousness.

The effects begin within 5 to 10 minutes and last several hours. The exact responses vary depending on the user's mood and situation.

RISKS

Accidents are more common, especially when driving, operating machinery, etc. Too much alcohol in one go can lead to fatal overdose or losing consciousness and choking on vomit. Alcohol is associated with violent behaviour. The lowering of inhibitions can make safer sex less likely. Alcohol can be dangerous mixed with other drugs. Long-term heavy use can lead to physical dependence and tolerance such that more is needed to get the same effect. Withdrawal from heavy use can lead to trembling and anxiety. High levels of use can also lead to heart, liver, stomach and brain damage.

REDUCING HARM

If someone is using alcohol they could:

1. Keep track of the amount consumed.
2. Not drive or operate dangerous machinery whilst under the influence.
3. Take a limited amount of cash with them when they go out.

4. Not get into too much round buying.

5. Remember the need for safer sex and always carry condoms.

6. Use non or low alcoholic drinks.

7. Agree limits with drinking partners.

8. Look out for friends when out drinking. At least one member of the party could stay sober.

9. Not take alcohol with other drugs, especially sedatives like tranquillizers, barbiturates, heroin and other opiates.

● ●

AMPHETAMINE

WHAT IS IT?
Amphetamine is a synthetic drug which comes in a variety of forms. These include a white, grey or yellowy powder, tablets and a liquid contained in a capsule. Street use of amphetamines is likely to be in powder form.

STREET NAMES
Amphet, speed, sulph, sulphate, uppers, wake ups, whites, whizz.

MEDICAL USE
Amphetamines were originally developed as medical drugs in the 1920s. They were widely prescribed in the 1950s and 60s to treat depression and sometimes as slimming pills. They were also given to soldiers to combat battle fatigue. Their current medical use is for narcolepsy (a tendency to fall asleep) and hyperkinesia (hyperactivity) in children, where the drug ritalin has been found to have a paradoxical effect in slowing down hyperactive youngsters.

HOW TAKEN
Amphetamine can be snorted up the nose in powder form.
As a powder, pills or capsules it can be taken by mouth,
sometimes mixed in a drink. Amphetamines are also occasionally smoked and quite commonly prepared for injection.

EXTENT OF USE
It has been estimated that between 5 and 10 per cent of
young British adults have used amphetamines.

EFFECTS
This is an 'upper' or stimulant drug which increases
breathing and pulse rate and increases energy and alert-
ness. A single dose can last 3–4 hours. Higher or repeated
doses can lead users to feel they have increased physical
and mental capacities. Sometimes after using amphetamines the user may feel anxious and restless and experience panic or feelings of persecution. These feelings wear
off once the user has stopped taking the drug.

Appetite tends to be suppressed and sleep delayed. This
explains the use of amphetamines by slimmers and people
who need to stay awake. Once the effect wears off users
can be very tired, needing some time to recover.

RISKS
The best known street name for amphetamine – speed –
highlights its main effect. The fact that it is a bit like bor-
rowed energy means that users will sometimes need time
to recover after a long session of use. They may find it difficult to stick to a normal work routine. It can also result in
users overdoing physical activity and possibly becoming
too hot and dehydrated, e.g. from all night dancing.

The strong upper effect can also be dangerous to people

with heart or blood pressure problems. Long-term use of amphetamines can result in tolerance developing (i.e. more being taken to get the same effect) and lack of food and sleep. This can reduce the user's resistance to illness. Some regular users get very panicky and feel they are being got at by other people.

Although physical dependence is not a problem, giving up long-term use can be very difficult as users can feel depressed and lethargic when not using the drug. They have come to rely on the lift that it gives them.

REDUCING HARM
If someone is using amphetamine they could:

1. Try to maintain normal work, diet and sleep routines, as far as possible.

2. Use a limited amount of the drug on an occasional basis and take breaks from use.

3. Allow enough time to recover from each session and let the body recharge its batteries.

4. Not overdo strenuous physical activity whilst using the drug.

5. If engaged in physical activity such as dancing or running, take breaks and drink lots of water to replace lost body fluids.

6. Be given reassurance and talked down if they become anxious.

7. If injecting amphetamines, take care to use clean equipment. Not share injecting equipment.

8. Not mix amphetamine with other drugs.

BARBITURATES

WHAT ARE THEY?

These are synthetic drugs manufactured for medical use in the treatment of anxiety and depression and as sleeping tablets. They have been manufactured since 1903 and there are many different types. They include Quinalbarbitone (Seconal), Amylobarbitone (Amytal), Tuinal (a combination of Seconal and Amytal), Pentobarbitone (Nembutal), and Butobarbitone (Soneryl). There are also slow-acting barbiturates like Phenobartitone, used to treat epilepsy. They are manufactured in the form of tablets, ampoules, suppositories, coloured capsules or sometimes syrup.

STREET NAMES

Barbs, barbies, blue bullets, blue devils, gorillas, nembies, pink ladies, red devils, sleepers.

MEDICAL USE

The prescribing of barbiturates was very common in the 1960s and 1970s, especially as sleeping pills. However UK prescriptions fell from 16 million in 1966 to just over one million in 1988. Barbiturate prescribing has been replaced in most cases by the prescribing of tranquillizers.

HOW TAKEN

Medical use is usually by mouth. Illicit users might take them by mouth but they are also prepared in solution for injection.

EXTENT OF USE

Medical prescribing has fallen dramatically. Those available for non-medical use are usually stolen from medical supplies. Quite common as street drugs in the late 1970s and early 1980s, their use is relatively rare today. There have been recent reports (1993) of them coming back into use.

EFFECTS

Barbiturates are sedative drugs which slow down the operation of the central nervous system. The effects are similar to alcohol and tranquillizers and last about 3–6 hours. A small dose will often make users feel relaxed and sociable – much the same effect as a few drinks. A large dose will have similar effects to being very drunk – slurred speech, loss of co-ordination and difficulty staying awake.

RISKS

The sedative effect can increase the risk of accidents, especially if someone is driving or operating machinery or falls over. High doses have also resulted in people becoming hostile, aggressive and having extreme reactions to people and situations.

There is a very high risk of overdose, which can be fatal. The lethal dose is quite close to the normal dose level and 10 pills may be enough to kill. The large number of accidental but fatal overdoses on medically prescribed barbiturates resulted in a large decrease in their medical use in the 1970s. Fatal overdose was also quite common amongst street users in the 1970s and early 1980s. The danger of accidents and overdose is greatly increased if barbiturates are used in combination with alcohol.

Tolerance and dependency can develop quickly with regular use of barbiturates. Anyone trying to stop abruptly after regular use of high doses can suffer severe withdrawal and may go into epileptic-type fits. With very high regular doses sudden withdrawal can be fatal. Most stories about the horrors and dangers of drug withdrawal are gross exaggerations. But with barbiturates the risks are real – and much greater than with opiate drugs like heroin.

Heavy users of barbiturates commonly suffer from bronchitis and pneumonia as the cough reflex is suppressed by the drug. Hypothermia can also be a problem in regular users.

Injecting barbiturates presents additional risks. Beside the usual risks of injecting (abscesses and infection from hepatitis or HIV if equipment is shared) it may be difficult to control dose levels, making overdose more likely.

Overall, it is apparent that barbiturates are really quite nasty drugs. Most drug workers – and certainly the authors – view them as potentially the most dangerous drugs in use. Happily, their use is now rare but the few signs of a renewed interest in them is worrying.

REDUCING HARM

If someone is using barbiturates they could:

1. Only use in the short term.
2. Avoid using with other drugs, especially alcohol or other sedatives.
3. Not drive or operate machinery whilst under the influence.
4. Take particular care with how strong a dose is. The danger of accidental overdose is very real.
5. Be aware of tolerance and possibly increasing doses over time.
6. Be aware of possible dependence with regular use.
7. If injecting, take great care with quantities used and avoid the sharing of injecting equipment with others.
8. If using regularly, be aware of possible bronchitis, pneumonia and hypothermia, and take care with diet, heating and health.

CAFFEINE

WHAT IS IT?
Caffeine is a drug found in tea, coffee, cocoa, many soft drinks such as cola, some chocolate and some medical tablets.

MEDICAL USE
Caffeine has been used in various medical preparations, for example, to ease headaches and to ease passing of water.

HOW TAKEN
Swallowed in a drink or eaten in confectionery or in pill form.

EXTENT OF USE
Most adults and many youngsters use caffeine on a daily basis.

EFFECT
Caffeine is an 'upper' or stimulant drug. It combats drowsiness and tiredness. It can also aid concentration. Its use increases heart rate and blood pressure. The effects start quickly and can last for a few hours. Using caffeine makes people urinate more. High doses can result in headaches and irritability.

RISKS
Regular, high dosage users of caffeine usually become dependent. Those taking more than about six to eight cups of instant coffee or tea a day may well experience withdrawal symptoms if they try to give up the drug. Going without the drug can lead to symptoms such as feeling

irritable, tiredness and headaches. Dependence on caffeine is usually socially acceptable.

Heavy, long-term use may increase risk of peptic ulcers, kidney, bladder and heart disease and blood pressure problems.

REDUCING HARM
If someone is using caffeine they could:

1. Try decaffeinated or lower strength tea and coffee products as well as herbal teas, etc.

2. Keep a record of the amount consumed and set daily limits.

3. Take a break from use on one or two days a week.

● ●
CANNABIS

WHAT IS IT?
Cannabis comes from the *Cannabis sativa* plant which grows all over the world. Whilst most of it is imported into the UK there is also some home-grown cannabis. The leaves from the plant (known as grass, bush, weed, etc.) can be smoked or eaten, or the drug can be concentrated into a resin block or oil form.

STREET NAMES
Bhang, black, blast, blow, Bob Hope, bush, dope, draw, ganja, grass, hash, herb, marijuana, pot, puff, resin, rocky, rope, sensi, skunk, sputnik, wacky backy, weed, zero zero (or double zero) and many other names. Some of the street names for cannabis are based on the country of origin, e.g. Afghan, Colombian, Lebanese, Moroccan, etc.

A 'J', 'joint', 'reefer' or 'spliff' is a cannabis cigarette made with cigarette papers. A 'roach' is the filter which is often made up of a rolled up piece of card.

MEDICAL USE

There has been no official medical use in the UK although cannabis can be used in the treatment of glaucoma and to relieve the side-effects of chemotherapy used in cancer treatment. Recently a cannabis substitute was prescribed to help alleviate the effects of multiple sclerosis (MS). It is widely used as a folk remedy in various parts of the world and was commonly used in this way in Victorian Britain.

HOW TAKEN

Herbal cannabis can be smoked by itself or with tobacco in a cigarette or pipe. The resin can be smoked and is sometimes eaten. Both resin and herbal forms are also sometimes cooked into dishes. Cannabis oil is usually coated on cigarette papers and smoked with tobacco.

EXTENT OF USE

Cannabis is the most widely used illegal drug in the UK. It has been estimated that there are over a million regular users, with many more having used it in the past.

EFFECTS

The effects of cannabis are often dependent on the user's moods and expectations. It can make people more relaxed, giggly and talkative and can enhance appreciation of sound and colour. It can also sometimes make users anxious and nervy, especially if they are uneasy to start with. Cannabis use affects concentration, thinking and manual skills. Feelings of hunger and forgetfulness are common. The effects start quickly and can last several hours.

RISKS

There is no danger of fatal overdose or physical dependency. As with any drug, psychological dependence can develop. If the user becomes reliant on the drug to help with relaxation it can become difficult to do without. Long-term heavy smoking of cannabis may lead to lung disorders. There is also a risk of accidents whilst under the influence, especially whilst driving. Using cannabis can make practising safer sex more difficult as it tends to lower inhibitions. Taking high doses whilst feeling depressed or anxious can lead to paranoia. Some people say this is more common with certain stronger types of cannabis such as sensimilia – a strong herbal form.

REDUCING HARM

If someone is using cannabis they could:

1. Avoid driving or operating dangerous machinery whilst under the influence.

2. Remember the need to practise safer sex – always carry condoms.

3. Take care where it is used. About 20,000 people are arrested each year in the UK for the illegal possession of cannabis and get a criminal record or at least a warning.

4. Be given reassurance if feeling anxious or paranoid under the influence.

5. Have a few days off from using every week. This will prevent any psychological dependence creeping up unawares.

6. Not eat large lumps of cannabis. This can be very disorientating as too much can be taken in one go.

COCAINE AND CRACK

WHAT IS IT?
Cocaine is derived from the coca shrub from South America. It is first made into coca paste then refined to produce cocaine, which is usually a white crystalline powder. Crack is so-called 'freebase' cocaine and is a smokeable form of cocaine. This comes in small lumps or 'rocks'.

STREET NAMES
Cocaine is known as C, Charlie, coke, dust, gold dust, lady, snow, white. A 'line' is a line of cocaine powder ready for sniffing. Crack is known as base, freebase, gravel, ice and rock.

MEDICAL USE
Cocaine is rarely used in medicine today. In the past it was used as a local anaesthetic. Until 1904 Coca Cola contained small quantities of extract of coca and was marketed as a tonic.

HOW TAKEN
Cocaine powder is usually sniffed up the nose, often through a rolled banknote or straw, but is sometimes made into a solution and injected. Cocaine freebase (crack) is smoked in a pipe, glass tube, plastic bottle or on foil. The smoke from the heated rocks is inhaled.

EXTENT OF USE
Its use is patchy in the UK. The price is high and it has been considered by many as a rich person's drug. In the United States there has been an epidemic of crack use amongst poor urban drug users. Despite many dire predictions a similar epidemic has yet to happen in the UK.

EFFECTS
This is a stimulant drug which can make users feel alert, confident and strong. At higher dose levels it can also make users feel anxious and panicky.

The effects come on strongly within 5–10 minutes but die away quickly. The dose needs repeating about every 20 minutes to maintain the effect.

RISKS
Large doses can make users feel very anxious. The stimulant effect can be followed by feelings of depression and fatigue. Although cocaine is not a drug that normally results in physical dependence, users can be tempted into regular use in an attempt to maintain feelings of energy and power and avoid depression and 'lack of go'. Heavy, regular use can result in restlessness, nausea, insomnia and paranoia. Repeated sniffing can damage the nasal passages. Repeated smoking can lead to wheezing and loss of voice. Injecting carries risks of infection by blood-borne viruses such as HIV and hepatitis if injecting equipment is shared.

REDUCING HARM
If someone is using cocaine or crack they could:

1. Try to avoid too frequent regular use.
2. Keep a record of the amounts taken and the costs involved and set limits.
3. Sniff cocaine rather than smoke crack.
4. Maintain regular sleep and diet patterns.
5. Allow recovery time from each session of use. Have a day or two off from use every week.
6. Avoid injecting if possible but otherwise take care not to share injecting equipment.
7. Not mix cocaine with other drugs (especially heroin and other depressants).

●●●●●●●●●●●●●●●●●●●●●●●●●●●●●●●●●●●●●
ECSTASY

WHAT IS IT?
Ecstasy is an illegally manufactured drug in tablet or capsule form. The chemical name is MDMA -3,4 methylenedioxymethamphetamine.

STREET NAMES
Adam, big brownies, burgers, California sunrise (also sometimes LSD), Dennis the Menace, disco biscuits, doves, E, Edward, essence, fantasy, love doves, M and Ms, M25s, MDMA, New Yorkers, rhubarb and custard, shamrocks, white doves, X, XTC and many others.

MEDICAL USE
It was originally manufactured in Germany in the early twentieth century as an appetite suppressant. There is no current medical use, although some doctors have suggested it could be used for those with long-term mental health problems.

HOW TAKEN
Ecstasy is usually swallowed as tablets or capsules.

EXTENT OF USE
It has become very popular amongst young people since 1988. There are recent estimates of up to 500,000 regular users in the UK.

EFFECTS
This is a stimulant drug with mild hallucinatory properties. It tends to make users feel more energetic. Many users report calmness, loss of anger and hostility, empathy with

others and an enhanced sense of communication. There can also be a heightened sense of surroundings and sound appreciation.

Sometimes users can feel nausea and disorientation. Clenching of the jaw and loss of appetite is common. The effects start after 20–60 minutes and can last for a number of hours.

RISKS

With high doses anxiety and confusion can result, especially if users are already panicky. Regular users can experience sleep problems, lack of energy and depression.

Whilst physical dependency is not a problem, psychological dependency on the feelings of calmness and euphoria associated with the use of the drug can develop. Little is yet known about the physical effects of long-term heavy use.

There is an increased danger of accidents whilst under the influence. There is also a problem of identification. Ecstasy can be difficult to distinguish from other drugs. Users are sometimes unsure about what drugs they are taking. LSD and amphetamine have both been sold as ecstasy. Many other so-called 'E tablets' have been found to contain no ecstasy and a variety of other home-made drugs or adulterants (see also ketamine, below).

Safer sex may be more difficult under the influence, especially with ecstasy's 'love drug' image. There have been some deaths both in the UK and in the United States. These have usually been connected with non-stop physical activity whilst under the influence leading to overheating and dehydration. Ecstasy use may be particularly dangerous for people who have heart or blood pressure problems.

REDUCING HARM

If someone is using ecstasy they could:

1. Avoid regular use.

2. Take care what is being used. Many tablets contain other drugs and adulterants.

3. If unsure about the strength of the drug, not take a full tablet. See what happens with half a tablet or smaller amounts first rather than going straight to full or multiple tablets.

4. Avoid too much continuous strenuous physical activity such as dancing non-stop. Take breaks and drink water to replace lost body fluids (not alcohol – it dehydrates even more).

5. Be reassured and talked down if they become disturbed.

6. Avoid driving or operating dangerous machinery whilst under the influence.

7. Not use with other drugs, especially alcohol.

8. Remember to practise safer sex and always carry condoms.

● ●

HEROIN (AND OTHER OPIATES)

WHAT IS IT?
Heroin is a powder derived from the opium poppy. There are also many other opiate-type drugs which are manufactured from synthetic chemicals.

OTHER OPIATES
These include codeine, diconal, dihydrocodeine (DF 118s), methadone, morphine, opium, palfium, pethidine and temgesic.

STREET NAMES
Boy, China white, dragon, gear, H, Harry, horse, Jack, junk, scat, skag, smack.

The names for other opiates include dike, DFs, dollies, meths, M, morf, palf, phyamps, etc.

MEDICAL USE
There is extensive medical use of opiates. Heroin itself is still prescribed as a strong pain reliever for terminally ill cancer patients. Other opiates are widely used for pain relief, as cough suppressants, anti-diarrhoea treatments, etc. Methadone is frequently prescribed as a treatment for heroin dependence. The aim is to supply a slow-acting heroin-like drug which does away with the need for the user to seek out street supplies of their drug. Occasionally heroin is itself prescribed for drug users, but these days this is very rare.

HOW TAKEN
Heroin can be smoked, sniffed or injected. Most other opiates are taken orally in tablet or liquid form. Tablets can be crushed and made into a solution for injection.

EXTENT OF USE
Heroin is the most commonly used illicit opiate. The number of users of heroin on a regular basis in the UK has been estimated at 100,000, but no one knows the exact figure. Other opiates are prescribed and sometimes used illegally.

EFFECTS
Opiates are sedative drugs. They slow down body functioning and give a feeling of warmth. Use is followed by feelings of relaxed detachment, removal of feelings of anxiety and blocking of feelings of physical and emotional pain.

Higher doses can result in sedation and drowsiness. Effects start quickly and can last several hours, but this varies with how the drug is taken.

RISKS
With regular use tolerance develops (more is needed to get the same effects) and physical dependence can result. Withdrawal after regular heavy use can produce unpleasant symptoms like a severe bout of 'flu.

Large doses can result in coma and possibly death. It is difficult to know sometimes just how much is being taken, as street drugs like heroin can be mixed with sometimes dangerous adulterants and the strength can vary. Injecting will make this more serious, as well as putting users at risk of blood-borne infections such as HIV and hepatitis if sharing injection equipment.

REDUCING HARM
If someone is using heroin they could:

1. Avoid everyday use.
2. Be aware of the risks from variable strength and adulterants, especially if injecting.
3. Maintain a regular daily routine, sleep and diet patterns.
4. Smoke rather than inject.
5. Not share injecting equipment.
6. Have a clean break from use every few days. When returning to use later, remember that tolerance will have fallen off. Amounts previously taken safely could now lead to fatal overdose.
7. Not mix heroin with other drugs especially other depressants (including alcohol).
8. Seek alternatives such as a prescription of oral methadone if available.

LSD

WHAT IS IT?
This is an illegally manufactured drug called Lysergic Acid Diethylamide. Only very small quantities are needed to get an effect. It is usually made into impregnated paper squares, tablets or capsules.

STREET NAMES
A, acid, blotter, California sunrise (also sometimes ecstasy) cheer, dots, drop, flash, Gorbachovs, hawk, L, lightning flash, Lucy, micro dot, paper mushrooms, penguins, rainbows, rhubarb and custard, shamrocks, smilies, stars, strawberries sugar, tab, trips, tripper, window and many other names.

MEDICAL USE
There is no current medical use for LSD. Previously there was some medical prescribing to long-term mentally ill patients but this was abandoned as the effects were too unpredictable.

HOW TAKEN
LSD is usually swallowed as a capsule, pill or impregnated paper square.

EXTENT OF USE
LSD was very popular in the 1960s and 70s 'hippy' culture. It has recently come back into fashion with younger users. It is often taken these days at parties and raves alongside amphetamine and/or ecstasy. LSD tends to be used on an occasional basis rather than regularly.

EFFECTS

LSD is an hallucinogenic drug. A 'trip' begins about 30 minutes to an hour after taking it and can last up to 12 hours. The effects will vary depending on the person, their mood and the situation. There can be sight and sound distortions, the intensification of colours and changes in sense of time and place.

Some users report heightened awareness of themselves and other people and almost mystical experiences. Feelings of being outside the body are also common. Whilst an LSD trip can be exciting it can also be scary. A 'bad trip' can be very disturbing and include strong feelings of panic and being persecuted.

RISKS

Unpleasant reactions can include anxiety, depression, paranoia and feelings of persecution and encroaching madness. This may be dangerous if users are already depressed or suicidal.

Accidents from driving or operating machinery are possible after using the drug, as it will make concentration on any task difficult. There is no evidence of physical dependency or any danger of fatal overdose. There is a built-in incentive not to use too often as after a few days of continuous use further doses are ineffective without a few days' break.

There is no known physical damage from even long-term use, although some users report 'flashbacks', i.e. re-experiencing a 'trip' some time afterwards. This can be disturbing, especially when the user does not know what it is.

REDUCING HARM

If someone is using LSD they could:

1. Take care with the amount consumed. If unsure take a very small quantity and see what happens.

2. Avoid using LSD when feeling anxious or depressed.

3. Plan carefully in whose company it is used. Make sure that the situation is under control and comfortable before using.

4. Be talked down and reassured if they become disturbed.

5. Recognize that whilst flashbacks can be scary, they don't mean that they are going mad. Flashbacks will go away after a while.

MAGIC MUSHROOMS

WHAT ARE THEY?
They are hallucinogenic mushrooms which grow wild in many parts of the UK in autumn. The main type is liberty cap (*Psilocybe*) but fly agaric (*Amanita muscaria*) is also sometimes used.

STREET NAMES
Liberties, mushies.

MEDICAL USE
None.

HOW TAKEN
The mushrooms are eaten raw or sometimes after being dried out. They can also be cooked with and then eaten or made into a tea or infusion and drunk.

EXTENT OF USE

There is a lot of experimenting by young people every autumn. More liberty caps are used than fly agaric. Some local surveys have shown over 15 per cent of 16 year olds have tried them.

EFFECTS

This is a mild hallucinatory drug. Its effects vary depending on the person and their mood, the situation of use and the expectations of the users.

Effects begin after about half an hour and can last up to nine hours, depending on how many are taken. Users often laugh a lot and report feeling more confident. Higher doses give a mild 'trip' with visual and sound distortions. Some people feel nausea and experience vomiting and stomach pains.

RISKS

A bad 'trip' can be unpleasant and scary. The effects of such a trip can include nausea, vomiting and paranoia. There is an increased danger of accidents whilst under the influence. There is no evidence of physical dependence or physical harm from use. The fact that much more is needed to get the same effect from a repeat dose means users usually have a gap between using and do not use too often. One other real danger is taking the wrong type by mistake and being poisoned. The symptoms of food poisoning include nausea, stomach cramps, vomiting and diarrhoea. If this becomes severe, it is best to consult a doctor.

REDUCING HARM

If someone is using magic mushrooms they could:

1. Be certain that they know what they are taking. Many mushrooms are poisonous.

2. Control the number taken. Twenty liberty caps or
    three fly agarics will bring on effects in most cases.

3. Avoid fly agaric, whose effects are less predictable.

4. Avoid using mushrooms if they are feeling anxious
    or depressed.

5. Carefully plan whom they use with, how and where.
    Try to choose a calm, friendly situation with friends
    around to support them if they should become
    panicky.

6. Be talked down and reassured if they become
    disturbed.

●●●
NITRITES (POPPERS, LIQUID GOLD)

WHAT IS IT?
A gold-coloured liquid called amyl or butyl nitrite. It usually comes in a bottle or in small glass 'vials' containing the
liquid which are 'popped' open and the vapours inhaled
(giving the street name 'poppers').

STREET NAMES
Amyl, liquid gold, locker room, poppers, ram, rush, snap-
per, stag, stud, thrust, TNT.

MEDICAL USE
There is no current medical use. In the past nitrites were
used for relief of angina/chest pains. They do this by dilating
the blood vessels, allowing more blood to get to the heart.

HOW TAKEN
Vapours from the liquid are inhaled through the nose
and/or mouth.

EXTENT OF USE

Nitrites are widely available in clubs and from joke and sex shops and are fairly cheap.

EFFECTS

The effects start straightaway but only last a few minutes. The acceleration of heartbeat and rush of blood to the brain gives a 'rushing' feeling. Users often say they feel time is slowed down. Loss of balance is common and headaches and nausea can result. Users say that nitrites prolong orgasm and thus enhance sexual pleasure. Using nitrites also relaxes the anal sphincter, making the drug attractive to those who practise anal sex. It has also been claimed to prevent premature ejaculation in men.

RISKS

Users can lose consciousness, especially if they are involved in vigorous physical activity like dancing or running. Accidents are more likely whilst under the influence. Use of nitrites could lead to a heart attack in people who have blood pressure or heart problems. This drug also increases pressure within the eyeball and should not be used by people who have glaucoma.

Regular use can lead to skin problems around the nose and lips. There have been some reports of nitrites being involved in certain rare forms of skin cancer. There are also reports of fatalities when users have drunk the liquid neat rather than inhaling the vapour.

Using this drug can make safer sex more difficult to put into practice.

Use does not lead to physical dependence and there is no definite evidence of long-term health damage.

REDUCING HARM

If someone is using nitrites they could:

1. Never drink the liquid – only inhale the vapours.
2. Take care not to use when undertaking strenuous physical activity.
3. Not drive or operate machinery under the influence.
4. Avoid using if they have heart disease, blood pressure problems or glaucoma.
5. Remember to practise safer sex.

● ●
SOLVENTS (GLUE, GAS, AEROSOLS, ETC.)

Sometimes called 'glue sniffing'

WHAT ARE THEY?
A wide range of solvents and volatile substances such as aerosols and gases, often based on domestic and industrial products. In particular there are solvent-based glues, lighter fuels such as butane gas, aerosols, typewriter correcting fluids, nail varnish remover, petrol, dry cleaning fluids, etc.

MEDICAL USE
None. These substances are in widespread domestic and industrial use.

HOW TAKEN
The vapours given off by these substances are breathed in through the nose and/or mouth. In some cases the substance may be placed in a bag or put on a rag and then sniffed. In other cases it will be directly inhaled, e.g. aerosols squirted straight down the throat.

EXTENT OF USE

These substances are available in just about every household and many shops and workplaces. Large numbers of young people have experimented with solvents at least once. Some local surveys have estimated that in some areas 20 per cent of all the 15 year olds have experimented with them. There are outbreaks of sniffing in local areas often for a short time. It is much more popular in summer than in winter, usually as an outdoor activity.

EFFECTS

The effects are fast but shortlived – usually less than $3/4$ hour without a repeat dose. Breathing and heart rate slow. The effect is to feel light-headed and often dizzy. Some users feel dreamy and happy, but others say they feel sick and drowsy. Some users claim to see or hear things that are not there. As it wears off users feel drowsy and may experience a hangover.

RISKS

Accidents are more likely as users can become unsteady and disorientated. Solvent use can lead to loss of consciousness. In most cases users quickly come round but there have been deaths from users choking on their own vomit. There is a serious risk of suffocation if the substance is used by putting it in a large bag which is then put over the head.

When squirted straight down the throat aerosols and gases have resulted in instant deaths through heart failure or freezing of the airways. Long-term, very heavy use of some solvents can damage the brain, kidney and liver, but it is very rare for this to happen. In practice there are few long-term health problems. Most risks seem to be acute, i.e. short term.

Tolerance can develop such that more is needed to get the same effect. Physical dependence is not a problem but psychological dependence can develop in some cases.

REDUCING HARM
If someone is using solvents they could:

1. Never use solvents on their own.
2. Know first aid to help others if needed.
3. Keep one person sober to mind the others.
4. If using a 'glue bag', use a small one and not place it over the head.
5. Be aware that, in most cases, glue is probably less harmful than the alternatives like butane gas.
6. Avoid squirting aerosols or butane straight down the throat. (Squirting into a bag, onto a rag or up the sleeve before inhaling the fumes is less dangerous.)
7. Avoid use in dangerous environments where accidents are more likely (train tracks, roads, canal or river banks, derelict buildings, near busy roads, etc.).

• •
STEROIDS

WHAT ARE THEY?
Anabolic steroids are drugs which are similar to hormones which are in the human body as growth and development agents. They can be made from natural and synthetic sources.

OTHER NAMES
Common trade names include Dianabol, Durabolin, Nadrolone, Stanozolol.

MEDICAL USE

Anabolic steroids are used to treat anaemia, thrombosis and breast cancer and for protein build up after long periods of inactivity.

HOW TAKEN

They are usually swallowed as pills or injected. They are often taken in cycles of a few weeks using then a few weeks off.

EXTENT OF USE

It is unclear how widespread their use is. In addition to their medical use they seem to be freely available through some gyms, health clubs, sports clubs, etc. Recently there have been reports that younger people are starting to use steroids as part of muscle building to improve appearance when dancing.

EFFECTS

These drugs build up body weight and increase the size of muscles. They also can make users feel more aggressive and better able to perform strenuous physical activity.

RISKS

Heavy use can lead to physical harm such as liver abnormalities, water retention, high blood pressure, fertility problems in men, development of 'male' characteristics in females and growth problems in young users. Psychological dependence appears to be quite common. Users come to feel that they cannot perform well without steroids. Prolonged use of anabolic steroids can make users feel more aggressive and violent. If injected, there is the risk of blood-borne infections such as HIV and hepatitis if injecting equipment is shared. Injecting may also make it diffi-

cult to control the amount taken, so there is a risk of taking
too much.

REDUCING HARM
If someone is using steroids they could:

1. Be careful about the quantities used. Many users
   will not know much about this and need to find out.
2. Only use for short periods in strictly controlled ways.
3. Be aware of the risks of psychological dependence.
4. Be aware of the possible side-effects and seek
   medical advice if needed.
5. Take particular care if injecting by carefully
   managing quantities taken and avoiding the risks of
   infection by not sharing needles.

TOBACCO

WHAT IS IT?
Tobacco is the product of tobacco plants mainly grown in
Third World countries. The active drug is nicotine. Tobacco
is made into cigarettes, cigars, pipe tobacco and snuff.

STREET NAMES
Backy, fags, snout.

MEDICAL USE
None.

HOW TAKEN
Tobacco is usually smoked but can also be snorted up the
nose as snuff or chewed in the mouth.

EXTENT OF USE

About one third of British adults smoke cigarettes. The numbers have been falling, especially among males. The numbers of teenagers smoking has grown recently, with young females outnumbering young male smokers.

EFFECTS

The effects are very quick and one dose can last up to 30 minutes. Pulse rate and blood pressure increases. Regular users often say smoking a cigarette alleviates anxiety and stress, helps them concentrate and combats boredom. Some smokers also find it suppresses the appetite for food.

RISKS

Tolerance develops quickly so more is needed to get the same effect. Most users become dependent and feel restless, irritable and depressed if they stop. Regular, long-term users have much greater risk of lung and some other cancers, heart disease, circulatory problems, bronchitis and ulcers. In the UK over 100,000 people die each year from the effects of smoking.

There is also a risk of health damage to other people who are nearby and may inhale the fumes. This 'passive' use of the drug has been claimed to cause several hundred deaths each year.

REDUCING HARM

If someone is using tobacco they could:

1. Set a daily limit for smoking and stick to it.
2. Avoid smoking in front of people and in places with poor ventilation.
3. Use low tar/extra filter brands where possible.

4. Avoid people who smoke and places where people smoke.

5. Use substitutes for cigarettes, including substitute nicotine in other forms such as chewing gum and patches.

●●

TRANQUILLIZERS

WHAT ARE THEY?
These are synthetic drugs manufactured for medical use in the treatment of anxiety, depression, sleeplessness and epilepsy. They include minor tranquillizers such as Diazepam (Valium), Lorazepam (Ativan) and Chlorodiazepoxide (Librium) and sleeping tablets such as Nitrazepam (Mogadon), Flurazepam (Dalmane) and Euphynos (Temazepam). These drugs are collectively known as benzodiazepines.

STREET NAMES
Benzos, tranx. Mogadon are often called 'moggies'. Temazepam are called 'green or yellow eggs', 'jelly babies' or 'rugby balls'.

MEDICAL USE
Minor tranquillizers are mainly prescribed to relieve anxiety and some types are used as sleeping pills.

HOW TAKEN
They are usually taken as medicines, swallowed as pills or capsules. They are also used in same way on the street but some forms (especially temazepam) can be prepared for injection.

EXTENT OF USE
These are the most commonly prescribed drugs in the UK.

There were 23 million prescriptions for tranquillizers in 1988. In the UK 14 per cent of adults use them at some time in each year and 2.5 per cent use them regularly throughout the year. Twice as many females as males are prescribed these drugs. The extent of street use is unclear, but it has increased in recent years.

EFFECTS
These are sedative drugs. They slow down the operation of the central nervous system. They can make users drowsy and lethargic and possibly forgetful. They can relieve tension and anxiety and promote relaxation and calm. The effects begin after 10–15 minutes and can last up to six hours without repeating the dose.

RISKS
Slowing down reactions and causing drowsiness can increase the risk of accidents whilst under the influence. Tolerance develops quickly, so more is needed to get the same effect. Dependence can develop quickly with regular use. Withdrawal from the drug can lead to anxiety, headaches and nausea. After high doses sudden withdrawal can be dangerous and result in fits.

After a relatively short time these drugs can be ineffective in producing their desired effects. As tolerance to the drug develops there is the risk of increasing dependence by taking more and more of the drugs. These higher doses can lead to confusion, anxiety and forgetfulness.

Although it is not possible to overdose fatally on a benzodiazepine on its own, they are much more dangerous in combination with other drugs, particularly alcohol. They have been implicated in a number of fatal overdoses when mixed in this way.

REDUCING HARM

If someone is using tranquillizers they could:

1. Only use in the short term, if possible under good medical supervision.

2. Avoid repeat prescriptions.

3. Not use with other drugs, especially alcohol or other sedatives.

4. Not drive or operate machinery whilst under the influence.

5. Not withdraw suddenly if dependent. Seek medical help and a gradual withdrawal programme.

6. Seek alternative methods of dealing with anxiety or insomnia.

7. If injecting, take care with quantities and avoid sharing injecting equipment.

●●

OTHER DRUGS (KETAMINE, PCP AND 'OVER THE COUNTER' MEDICINES)

Ketamine

This drug recently (1992) found its way into the club and rave scene in major cities. It is a powder which is sniffed or a tablet. It is not yet widely used (1993).

Street names include K, special K and super K.

Ketamine has pain-killing effects and alters perception. Users report feelings of detachment and remoteness. At first it gives a rush of energy and an hallucinogenic effect, a bit like LSD. Little is known yet about the risks but it seems that tolerance and physical dependence are not a problem with ketamine.

Taking ketamine when feeling anxious or depressed could result in disturbing experiences. The pain-killing effect could also increase the risk of accidents. It is known that a large single dose can produce numbness and irregular muscle co-ordination. The risks of regular long-term use are not yet known.

One additional risk is not knowing what you are taking. Ketamine itself came on to the scene when people thought they were buying ecstasy. They then realized they were being given something else.

PCP – Phencyclidine

This is an hallucinogenic drug which has some similarities to LSD but also has anaesthetic properties. It is only rarely available or used in the UK. It is more common in America.

PCP can be sniffed as a powder, smoked, taken in tablet form and injected, although injection is rare. The effects are similar to those described above for ketamine, but PCP has an image of being a heavy drug where hallucinations and disorientation may be particularly severe.

American sources suggest that regular long-term use can lead to paranoia, violent behaviour, anxiety, depression and severe mood swings.

Over the counter (OTC) medicines

There are a number of medicines (cold remedies, cough syrups, travel sickness pills etc.) which are available without a prescription from chemists and which can be used to get a 'high'. Some of these drugs have opiate-like or sedative effects. Examples are 'Gee's Linctus', 'Benylin' cough mixture, 'Night Nurse' or 'Codis' tablets. Other OTC drugs have stimulant-type effects. Examples are 'Sudafed', 'Phenergan' or 'Do-Do' tablets. Some OTC medicines contain a mixture of stimulant and sedative drugs. One example is 'Day Nurse'.

Regular illegal drug users will sometimes resort to the use of OTC medicines if they cannot get their normal drug of choice. For example, heroin users might use some of the opiate-like OTC medicines.

Younger people might experiment with OTC medicines (or herbal remedies) to see if they can get a high. Rumours fly. 'Try some X and you'll get a buzz.' Sometimes the buzz comes and sometimes it's a let down. Young people are ever optimistic in the search for new excitement.

Appendix II

•••••••••••••••••••••••••••••••••

Where to find out more

•••••••••••••••••••••••••••••••••

•••

HELPING ORGANIZATIONS

In your locality

If you cannot find out which drug organizations and services exist in your local area, ring your Regional Health Information Service free on 0800 66 55 44. They will have details of all the health-related services in your area.

Alternatively, ring SCODA (Standing Conference on Drug Abuse) (071–928 9500), a national organization which keeps records of drug services all over the country.

National organizations

ADFAM National

5th floor
Epworth House
25 City Road
London EC1Y 1AA

Tel. 071–638 3700 (office and helpline)

The national charity for the families and friends of drug users. Runs a national helpline and provides training courses, including courses for parents.

Families Anonymous

Unit 37
Doddington and Rollo Community Association
Charlotte Despard Avenue
London SW1 5JE

Tel. 071–498 4680

Involved in support groups for parents and friends of drug users in different parts of the country.

Healthwise
    9 Slater Street
    Liverpool L1 4BW

    Tel. 051–707 2262

A regional health information service and national publisher of drug education materials for use in schools, with parents and young people.

ISDD (Institute for the Study of Drug Dependence)
    Waterbridge House
    32–36 Loman Street
    London SE1 0EE

    Tel. 071–928 1211

The main source of up-to-date information on drugs in the UK. They produce a range of pamphlets on drugs and the bimonthly *Druglink* magazine. Excellent library.

Narcotics Anonymous
    UK Service Office
    PO Box 198J
    London N19 3LS

    Tel. 071–498 9005

Network of self-help groups for drug users based on Alcoholics Anonymous model.

The Red Cross
    9 Grosvenor Street
    London SW1X 7EJ

    Tel. 071–235 5454

Release

388 Old Street
London EC1V 9LT

Tel. 071–729 9904;
24-hour helpline (071–603 8654) for emergencies.

Information and advice about legal and social aspects of drugs.

SCODA (Standing Conference on Drug Abuse)

Waterbridge House
32–36 Loman Street
London SE1 0EE

Tel. 071–928 9500

Advice and information about drugs and drug services.

St Andrew's Ambulance Association

St Andrew's House
Milton Street
Glasgow G4 0HR

Tel. 041–332 4031

St John's Ambulance Brigade

1 Grosvenor Crescent
London SW1X 7EF

Tel. 071–251 0004

TACADE

1 Hulme Place
The Crescent
Salford M5 4QA

Tel. 061–745 8925

They produce a range of drug and health education resources; also provide advice to teachers and others on health education issues.

Books and pamphlets to read

Coping with a Nightmare – Family Feelings about Long Term Drug Use (ISDD (see above)).
Based on interviews with families and parents about how they have reacted to long-term, heavy drug use by their youngsters.

Drugs and your Child (ISDD (see above)).
Pamphlet for parents covering basic information and advice.

Drugs in Perspective, M. Plant (Hodder and Stoughton, 1987).
Good, wide-ranging paperback.

Living with Drugs, M. Gossop (Temple Smith, 1982).
Excellent paperback covering social and historical aspects.

Street Drugs, A. Tyler (New English Library, 1988).
Very readable paperback crammed full of information.

Drug education resources of special interest to parents

The four resources listed below provide interesting and fun ways for parents and young people to learn about drugs together at home. They can all be obtained from Healthwise (Tel. 051–707 2262).

Drug Facts card game – test your knowledge and play a game with your youngsters. A fun way to learn up-to-date information.

Drug Fax computer game – works on any AMIGA or PC computer and has been specially designed for parents to use by themselves or with their youngsters.

Streetwise – new 'sex, drugs and rock 'n' roll' board
    game. It is based on making decisions about real-life
    moral dilemmas. Young people love playing it and it
    can be fun for all the family to play together.

XTC – A Parent's Guide to the Drug Ecstasy – audio
    tape of experts talking about young people's use of
    ecstasy and what parents can do.

Drugs education and training packs for use with groups

These packs are designed to be used in schools and youth
centres.

*Don't Panic – Responding to Incidents of Young
    People's Drug Use*
    (Available from Healthwise; Tel 051 707 2262)
    Reference, individual learning and training package
    focused on responding positively and sensitively to
    incidents of young people's drug use.

Ecstasy and Drug Use in the 1990s
    (Daniels; Tel. 0223 467144)
    Group exercises and factual information about the
    new drug scene among young people.

High Profile
    (ISDD: Tel. 071 – 430 1991/3)
    Newspaper-style drugs education resource with
    activities for youth and community workers to do
    with young people.

Taking Drugs Seriously
    (Healthwise: Tel. 051 – 707 2262)
    Comprehensive drugs education package covering
    facts, risk taking, attitudes, reducing harm, the law,
    giving and receiving help, etc. Includes workshop
    for parents.

INDEX

Numbers in *italic* refer to illustrations